INSIGHT GUIDES

Great Breaks

COTSWOLDS

Contents

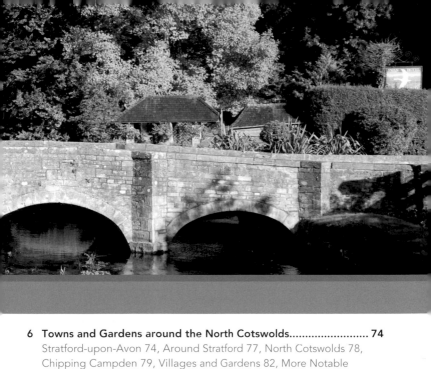

Travel Tips

The Cotswolds' Top 10

Here are just some of the highlights of this quintessentially English area of rural Britain, which is peppered with stone villages tucked into lush river valleys and graced with elegant, historic towns

▲ **Gloucester** *(p.21)*. Renowned for its sublime cathedral, other highlights include a fascinating waterways museum and historic docks.

▲ **Cheltenham** *(p.62)*. This town, which is noted for its specialist shopping, proudly shows off its Regency splendour, best seen in the Prom.

▲ **Westonbirt, The National Arboretum** *(p.28)*. The stunning arboretum was planted in the 19th century and is a celebration of trees from around the world.

▶ **Cirencester** *(p.48)*. Roman settlement meets 21st-century bustling market town. Visit the museum of Roman antiquities and then hit the speciality shops.

▼ Chipping Campden *(p.79)*. This is one of the most beautiful of the Cotswold small towns, with a totally unspoilt high street.

▲ Sudeley Castle *(p.66)*. A romantic setting for hundreds of years of history, Sudeley Castle is also renowned for its award-winning gardens.

▼ The Slaughters *(p.91)*. These two idyllic Cotswold villages are almost too beautiful to be true, pure architectural and rural bliss.

▲ Snowshill Manor *(p.69)*. All you could wish for from a typical Cotswold-stone manor house, surrounded by gardens inspired by the Arts and Crafts Movement.

▼ The Cotswold Way *(p.53)*. Stretching 102 miles (164km) along the Cotswold escarpment, this long-distance footpath can be joined at several points along the way.

▲ Stratford-upon-Avon *(p.74)*. For lovers of all things Shakespearean, the town is a shrine to the immortal bard.

Overview

Cotswolds' Rugged Harmony

To many people, the Cotswolds is the essence of England, a place where they would love to live – if not immediately, then certainly when they retire

Here in the Cotswolds the hills are high and wild, but rarely bleak, and simple stone cottages combine with church, manor house and tithe barn to create a picture of timeless beauty. Stone here is plentiful and

it is this stone that gives the region its character, creating a harmonious landscape of fields bounded by drystone walls, churches with majestic towers, opulent town houses, stately homes and humble cottages with lichen-patched walls beneath steeply pitched roofs of limestone tile.

LOCATION AND TOPOGRAPHY

Stone also defines the boundaries of the Cotswolds. The region's creamy white oolitic limestone constitutes a distinctive geological feature. The Cotswold Hills were formed from limestone created by the accumulation of shelly debris beneath the warm, shallow Midlands Sea that covered much of west-central England

in ancient geological times. This thick compressed raft of calcium carbonate was later thrust up by tectonic pressure to create a tilted sheet running southwest to northeast.

To the north, west and south this sheet forms a cliff-like escarpment running from Mickleton, near Stratford-upon-Avon, southwards to Wotton-under-Edge, near Bath. Walkers can follow the length of the escarpment along the Cotswold Way, a long-distance footpath designated in 1970. Its highest point, on Cleeve Hill, north of Cheltenham, rises to 1,040ft (317 metres). The edge is littered with prehistoric hillforts, burial mounds and the remains of ancient quarrying. The limestone grassland that tops these hills is rich in wild flowers, including rare orchids, which are festooned with butterflies.

Off the main roads you will descend into wooded valleys with houses clustered around village greens, ancient churches and welcoming pubs. Many of the settlements in the Cotswolds are tucked into hidden hollows and valleys

Above: rolling Cotswold landscape.
Below: Cotswold stone houses in Guiting Power.

Above: the tall spikes of the 'Cotswold Queen' Verbascum, growing in a cottage garden.

where they are invisible to anyone travelling on the high roads. The lanes here are narrow and twisty, often no more than a farm track, and it is advisable to have a detailed map to hand.

The prettiest Cotswold villages lie along the valleys of the Churn, Coln and Leach, the Eye, the Dikler and the Ampney Brook, the Windrush, the Frome and the many other brooks and streams that spring up in these hills to drain eventually into the Thames, Severn and Avon rivers. Many of these are misfit valleys (valleys that are very wide in proportion to the small streams that now flow through them), and were created by the meltwaters that flowed across the Cotswolds as the Midlands glaciers began to break up towards the end of the last Ice Age, 10,000 years ago.

Once the glaciers were gone, the streams shrank to a fraction of their original size and various settlements began to grow up along the sheltered valley sides. These provided natural terracing, fertile soils and shelter from the wind and snow of a harsh Cotswolds' winter. In several places in the Cotswolds you can still gain a real feel for the enclosed nature of the landscape, the sense of inhabiting a secret magic world cut off from the rest of civilisation.

ECONOMY

The Romans introduced the distinctive long-woolled breed of sheep known as the Cotswold Lions, on which the subsequent prosperity of the region was based. Cotswold wool had already gained a Europewide reputation by the 11th century, and by the 14th century it was being exported to Flanders, Spain and Italy. Wool wealth paid for the churches of the Cotswolds, the majestic abbeys (many, such as Cirencester, erased from the face of the earth during the 16th-century Dissolution of the Monasteries) and the fine houses of the merchants in Cirencester, Chipping Campden, Painswick and Northleach. The Cotswolds continued to be a centre for textile production well into the early 20th century, with mills lining the banks of fast-flowing streams at Blockley, Chalford, Stroud and Nailsworth.

Taxation, combined with competition from South America, Australia and New Zealand, caused the Cotswold sheep industry to go into sharp decline in the 19th century, and the Cotswold Lion breed was only just rescued from extinction by a small group of enthusiasts who formed the Cotswold Sheep Society in 1892. Today you can see Cotswold Lions and other rare breeds at the Cots-

⑤ Preserving the Beauty

Laurie Lee, author of *Cider with Rosie* (1959), was lucky enough to be born near Slad, in 1914, where he spent most of his life. In 1995, two years before he died, he led a campaign to prevent the construction of a housing estate in his precious 'jungly, bird-crammed, insect-hopping valley'. Lee observed that the Cotswolds was 'easy to take for granted until you went away and discovered that the whole world was nothing like so special'.

wold Farm Park, and see wool being spun and woven at the Cotswold Woollen Weavers.

The Cotswolds remains an agricultural region but it has also become glamorous through 'horsiculture', with the profitable sports of polo and eventing entrenched in the area, bringing the rich and famous. Landowners have been quick to capitalise on the phenomenon, with events throughout the summer at Cirencester Park, Badminton and Gatcombe Park, home to the Princess Royal. The novelist Jilly Cooper, who lives in Bisley, captured brilliantly this side of life in the Cotswolds in her comic novels *Polo*, *Riders*, *Rivals* and *Jump*.

Guide to Coloured Boxes

⑤ Eating	This guide is dotted
⑥ Fact	with coloured boxes providing
⑥ Green	additional practical and cultural infor-
⑥ Kids	mation to make the most of your visit.
⑥ Shopping	Here is a guide to
⑥ View	the coding system.

THE FUTURE OF THE COTSWOLDS

Another important aspect of the economy in the Cotswolds is tourism. It is a struggle to maintain a balance between protecting the natural habitats and preserving the villages and towns in the region *(see Conservation feature p.60)* and providing the thousands of visitors a year the infrastructure they require. Traffic and litter alone cause constant problems. In 2010, Cotswold District Council adopted a 'Going Green' policy to promote sustainable tourism in the area *(see p.119)*.

Without tourism, many regional businesses would die and the local economy struggle. With the effects of recession, many Britons are choosing to holiday at home. Although this will boost the Cotswolds' economy it will continue to put a strain on its survival as a unique environment.

Above: limestone rock formation known as The Devil's Chimney, on Leckhampton Hill.

Food and Drink

There has been a renaissance in the use of local produce in reputable eating establishments throughout the Cotswolds. Add to this the growth of microbreweries and the region's first vineyard, and food and drink continue to reach higher standards.

WHAT TO EXPECT

In recent years the Cotswolds has seen a proliferation of high-quality food in top-class restaurants, innovative pubs and traditional teashops. Indeed, teashops are a mainstay of the region and there are some exceptional ones – try Tisanes *(see p.73)* in Broadway or Badgers Hall *(see p.85)* in Chipping Campden. The emphasis is on seasonal, local food, showcased in a variety of ways, from traditional pub grub to Michelin-standard restaurant menus. Some places can be very expensive but establishments throughout the region serve tasty and unpretentious food at perfectly reasonable prices.

LOCAL PRODUCE

Many pubs and restaurants serve organically produced meat – Gloucester Old Spot pork is undergoing a revival

Above: a traditional inn serving food and drink in the village of Broadway.

F Food Festivals

There are plenty of food festivals throughout the year; here are just a few to whet the appetite:
February – Bite Festival at Chipping Campden. Food fairs, farmers' markets, chef demos and more.
June – Cheltenham Food and Drink Festival, which brings producers in from across the country, plus local contributors and celebrity chefs; Asparafest in the Vale of Evesham, an extravaganza where asparagus is the star.
September – Stroud Food Festival – artisan produce at its best; Stratford-upon-Avon Food Festival – check out the Great Tastes Markets; Tetbury Food and Drink Festival, bringing together the best of Cotswold produce.

and Prince Charles's Highgrove estate is just one local source of organic beef, lamb and pork. Jesse Smith's butcher's shop *(see p.49)* in Cirencester also supplies first-class produce. Market gardening, particularly in the Vale of Evesham, has been an important part of the local economy for centuries, with festivals that take place in honour of certain vegetables and fruit.

Much of the local produce ends up in the excellent farmers' markets held in the region. One of the best is at Stroud – the biggest market of its kind in the country, and named Best Farmers Market in the UK in 2013. There are between 45 and 60 stalls set up every Saturday (9am–2pm) offering organic, free range and locally produced food. In addition there are cooked foods to eat on site or take away. To find other markets, check www.cotswold.gov.uk.

The Cotswolds has a few regional speciality dishes. One is Gloucestershire Squab Pie – unlike squab pie from other regions that uses young pigeon, this one is made from lamb or mutton. Special recipe Tewkesbury mustard has been made there since the 17th century.

DAIRY PRODUCTS

You will find excellent dairy products in the Cotswolds, from home-made ice creams and yoghurts to local cheeses such as Single and Double Gloucester (produced since the 16th century) and North Cerney goat's cheese. Other local artisan cheeses include the Cotswold versions of brie and cheddar. The Simon Weaver Cotswold Organic Dairy at Upper Slaughter produces three organic Cotswolds bries, plain, blue-veined and herb, all made using milk from their Friesian herd. Ice cream is lovingly made using organic milk in the Italian *gelato* style by The Cotswold Ice Cream Company. Winstones of Bownham, near Stroud, have been producing delicious ice cream since 1925 and also make frozen yoghurt and sorbets.

BEER, WINE AND SOFT DRINKS

There's been a huge resurgence of small, independent breweries producing a wonderful and astoundingly diverse range of ales. However, there are some breweries that have been in business for years, such as the Donnington Brewery at Upper Sewell, where the Arkell family started brewing in 1865. The Hook Norton Brewery near Chipping Norton has been producing beer in the traditional method since 1849. The Stroud Brewery, in business for 250 years, moved to larger prem-

Above: Cotswold brewery using Shire horses to deliver beer to local pubs.

ises in 2011 enabling them to produce organic bottled beer. A recent artisan brewer is the Cotswold Lion Brewery (2012), at Coberley, producing three first-rate tipples, Shepherd's Delight, Best in Show and Golden Fleece.

In Dodington Ash, the Cotswold Spring Brewery uses natural spring water from the limestone plateau of the Cotswold Hills to produce its additive-free ale, while the Cotswold Spring Water Company, also in Dodington, bottles this same mineral water to sell to the public. For pure, non-alcoholic fruit juices one of the best in the region is Bensons of Sherborne. The Cotswolds' first vineyard was planted at Poulton Hill near Cirencester in 2010, with the first wines due in 2014.

Find our recommended restaurants at the end of each tour. Below is a Price Guide to help you make your choice.

Eating Out Price Guide

Two-course meal for one person, including a glass of wine.

£££	over £30
££	£15–30
£	under £15

Tour 1

Gloucester and the Vale of Berkeley

This 35-mile (56km) drive is a full-day's sightseeing, taking in castles and nature reserves, travelling through mostly flat terrain alongside canals, then ending up in Gloucester

Lying between the River Severn to the west and the steep Cotswold escarpment to the east, this tour begins in the Vale of Berkeley (also known as Berkeley Vale), an area of rich pasture and small dairy farms. Red-brown Gloucester cows (now a rare breed that can be seen at the Cotswold Farm Park; see p.93) were once raised here to produce creamy Single and Double Gloucester cheeses.

As the tour continues there is the opportunity to learn more about the important canal restoration work that is being carried out in the area, and finally to explore Gloucestershire's county town.

Highlights

- Berkeley Castle
- Slimbridge Wildfowl and Wetlands Centre
- Frampton-on-Severn
- Saul Junction Heritage Centre
- Hardwicke Court
- Gloucester

BERKELEY

The starting point of the tour is **Berkeley Castle ❶** (tel: 01453-810 332; www.berkeley-castle.com; May–Sept Sun–Wed 11am–5pm, Apr and Oct Sun only; charge), the site where Edward II was brutally murdered in

two table tombs of lesser mortals in the churchyard. One marks the burial place of England's last court jester (died 1728), whose grave bears an epitaph penned by Jonathan Swift; while the other has an equally witty engraving summing up the life of local watchmaker Thomas Pearce (died 1665).

Detour for the Children

On leaving the castle head west for the centre of town, or east to **Cattle Country Adventure Park** (Berkeley Heath Farm; tel: 01453-810 510; www.cattlecountry.co.uk; June–Aug daily 10am–5pm, Mar–May, Sept–Oct Sat–Sun 10am–4pm, with exceptions; charge). Children will enjoy its farm trail (complete with roaming bison), steam train ride, indoor playbarn, boating lake and outdoor assault course with zip wires and a vertical drop slide.

Dr Jenner's House

In the centre of Berkeley, the remarkable story of Edward Jenner's research and the development of the

1327. Despite being a party to regicide, the lords Berkeley managed to hang on to their magnificent feudal castle, which has passed through 24 generations of the same family from 1153 to the present day. The castle looks the part, with its massive Norman keep (built 1067), the cell where Edward spent his last days and the Great Hall, where the English barons held their last meeting before riding to Runnymede to force King John to set his seal to the Magna Carta.

Eight acres (3 hectares) of fine terraced gardens surround the castle, including Queen Elizabeth I's bowling green and the 8th Earl's swimming pool. A **Butterfly House** (May–Sept; charge) is located in the walled kitchen garden, where tropical species fly freely and where you can see the entire life cycle of transition from chrysalis to butterfly. In St Mary's Church alongside the castle, fine alabaster effigies commemorate the Berkeleys and their wives, but it is worth seeking out the

Above: a butterfly feasting in Berkeley Castle's Butterfly House.

⑤ An End to Smallpox

In the 18th century, local doctor Edward Jenner noted in the course of his work that the milkmaids who contracted cowpox, a minor disease, became immune to smallpox, a disease that killed thousands of children every year and left thousands more blinded or scarred for life. In 1796 Jenner vaccinated a local boy with cowpox, and thus invented the science of immunology, as well as the practice of vaccination.

world's first vaccine (*see box, above*) is told through films and displays at the **Dr Jenner's House** (The Chantry, Church Lane; tel: 01453-810 631; www.jennermuseum.com; Mar–Oct Sun–Fri noon–5pm; charge). Laid out in Jenner's country home, the exhibits include 18th-century cartoons satirising Jenner and his patients as

bovine country buffoons. Set in the grounds is a 19th-century cider- and ale-house. Jenner does not enjoy the regard that you might expect in England, a point illustrated by the fact that this fascinating museum was paid for by a Japanese philanthropist.

RIVERS AND CANALS

From the centre of Berkeley, bear right through Market Place to Maybrook Street and on to Station Road. Cross a small roundabout then, just after you pass through Wanswell, turn right to reach the northern tip at Purton. **Purton ②** is a peaceful spot with a pretty church (1874) on the Gloucester and Sharpness Canal, where boats pass through a swing bridge observed by picnickers and passing tourists. There are fine walks along the towpath as far as Gloucester.

Sharpness Detour

Before reaching Purton, a detour west takes you to the Severnside port

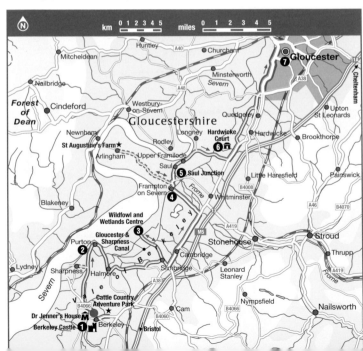

town of **Sharpness**, with its busy container terminal. The town was founded in 1794 when the Gloucester and Sharpness Canal was dug so that ships could sail directly to Gloucester without having to navigate the difficult tidal waters of the River Severn. The canal remains in use, and is capable of taking ships as large as 1,000 tonnes. Sharpness is also the centre of the local elver fishing industry. Elvers are young eels that are carried by the Gulf Stream from the Sargasso Sea, where they hatch, to the rivers of northern Europe, where they grow to adults, before returning to the Sargasso to breed and die. The elvers are netted along these banks between February and May. Rumours that elvers are dying out in the River Severn have led to bylaws being laid down to regulate elver net fishing.

Wildfowl and Wetlands Centre

From Purton continue following signs south all the way to Slimbridge. You will encounter the canal again if you visit **Slimbridge**, for the road to the **Wildfowl and Wetlands Centre** ❸ (tel: 01453-891 900; www.wwt.org.uk/slimbridge; daily Apr–Oct

Above: an old jetty juts out into the River Severn at the port town of Sharpness.

9.30am–5.30pm, Nov–Mar 9.30am–5pm; charge) passes over one of several bridges that swing aside to let ships and pleasure boats through. The centre was founded in 1946 by the artist and naturalist Sir Peter Scott on a marshy site beside the Severn, which naturally attracts large numbers of wild birds. These can be seen from hides dotted discreetly around the margins of the site, while the ponds around the reserve are home to a great array of wildfowl from all over the world. From the entrance the route passes through a visitor centre with displays explaining the ecology

Ⓖ Saving the Crane

Due to hunting and draining of the wetlands the crane became extinct in the UK about 400 years ago. Now these elegant birds could again be a common feature across Britain thanks to a project introduced at Slimbridge Wildfowl and Wetlands Centre. It is vital that young cranes don't knowingly come into contact with humans so the chicks are hand reared and taught the skills needed to survive in the wild by experts disguised as adult cranes.

Above: a Demoiselle Crane at the Wildfowl and Wetlands Centre.

of wetland habitats around the world (*see box p.17*).

Before leaving the Slimbridge area, take the chance to visit the village church, an unusually complete example of the 13th-century Early English style, with fine foliated capitals and an unusual lead font dating from 1664. From the church continue east to meet the A38 and head north towards Gloucester.

Frampton-on-Severn

Four miles (6.5km) north on the A38, turn left for **Frampton-on-Severn** ❹, (B4071), set around England's largest village green. Formerly a marsh and still dotted with bird-filled ponds, the green was created in the early 18th century when Richard Clutterbuck, a wealthy official at the Bristol Customs House, built **Frampton Court**, the huge Palladian building visible behind the high wall to the east of the green (the Gothic revival-style Orangery of 1743 is more easily seen). In the mid-1980s, 300 19th-century watercolours of local wild flowers were found in the court's attics and were published as

Above: Slimbridge's 13th-century church, St John the Evangelist.

The Frampton Flora. Today guided tours of this fine historic house are available and you can enjoy bed-and-breakfast in rooms with beautiful views over the grounds and lake (tel: 01452-740 267, 01452-740 268 to book tours and accommodation).

On the opposite side of the green are charming timber houses, including Frampton Manor (also known as Manor Farmhouse), a fine 12th- to 16th-century building with a delightful garden (tel: 01452-740 268; house and gardens by appointment all year). The manor is reputed to be the birthplace of 'Fair Rosamund' Clifford (died 1176), the celebrated mistress of Henry II. Just beyond the manor is the church, which has a notable late 12th-century Romanesque lead font depicting the Evangelists.

Nature Detour

Four miles (6km) further on from Frampton at Arlingham, set in a loop of the River Severn, **St Augustine's Farm** (tel: 01452-740 277; www.st augustinesfarm.co.uk; Mar–Oct Thu–Sun 11am–5pm, closed 1–12 July;

Above: fishing on the green at Frampton-on-Severn, with Frampton Court Orangery in the background.

Above: one of the half-timbered houses lining the south side of the green in Frampton-on-Severn.

charge) allows children to make friends with rabbits, goats, hens and calves and watch the organic dairy herd being milked. One mile (1.6km) west is the site of an important prehistoric river crossing used by Welsh cattle drovers until quite recent times. Now twitchers come here to watch wading birds.

Saul Junction

From Frampton village green, at the crossroads take the road opposite and continue to follow signs to Saul Junction. **Saul Junction 5** is located halfway along the Gloucester and Sharpness Canal, where it meets the Stroudwater Canal. The road here crosses Sandfield Bridge, which is hydraulically operated by the British Waterways bridge keepers. As well as providing information about the restoration of the Cotswold Canals, the **Heritage Centre** (tel: 07854-026 504; weekends and bank holidays only 12.30–4pm) also arranges boat trips aboard the narrow boat *Perseverance* (Easter–Sept; charge).

The Stroudwater Canal was constructed between 1775 and 1779 from the River Severn at Framilode to Wallbridge near Stroud to bring coal to the prosperous Stroud woollen industry. The Gloucester and Sharpness Canal was built in 1827, and a disused junction lock added in 1820 to enable the two canals to meet at one level is still visible here. Sadly most of the Stroudwater Canal is not navigable,

Above: Saul Junction on the Gloucester and Sharpness Canal is a mecca for narrow boaters.

Above: the late-Georgian Hardwicke Court was designed in neoclassical style by Sir Robert Smirke, architect of the British Museum.

ⓥ Severn Bore

The Severn Bore is a large wave up to 9.8ft (3 metres) in height and moving at a speed of up to 13mph (21kph) – fast enough to attract surfers in search of a challenge – which travels up the River Severn estuary to Gloucester. The bore can be seen at regular intervals throughout the year; best viewing spots are from the back lanes that thread the Vale of Framilode north of Saul Junction.

Above: surfers riding the Severn Bore in the early morning sunshine.

but a restoration programme is in place to restore it to its former glory. Beside Sandfield Bridge is an excellent café called The Stables.

From Saul Junction continue north to the junction and turn right. As the road veers east away from the River Severn, just after the Anchor Inn, take Castle Lane on the right, which crosses the canal again, to join the A38 and continue on to Gloucester.

HARDWICKE COURT

Another spot to seek out as you head for Gloucester is **Hardwicke Court** ❻ (tel: 01452-720 212; Easter–Oct Mon 2–4pm, gardens 2–5pm; charge), which lies on the west side of the A38 south of the village of Hardwicke itself. The building is not signposted so you will need to keep your eyes open. Built in 1816–17 by Sir Robert Smirke for the Lloyd-Baker family, the house is of great interest architecturally. When it is open you can visit the pleasant reception rooms with their fine family portraits. Continue on the A38 for approximately 5 miles (8km) to reach the centre of Gloucester.

GLOUCESTER

Gloucester ❼ is not one of England's most beautiful cities, though it is a place of enormous historical interest. The city was founded by the Romans shortly after the invasion in AD 43 as a temporary encampment for the XXth Legion, which moved to permanent headquarters at Caerleon, in Wales, in AD 75. Gloucester then became a *colonia* (a settlement for retired army veterans), and from this point it grew to become a major Saxon town, with a mint and a monastery. William the Conqueror held court here and it was here, in 1085, that he ordered the Domesday Book to be compiled. By the 16th century, Gloucester had also become a major port, shipping corn, timber, slate, metals, wines and spirits.

Historic Waterfront

Gloucester's docklands area has been transformed with a mixture of housing, shops and restaurants and several attractions housed in former 19th-century warehouses around the dock basin. Around the site many original features have been retained, including rail tracks, mooring rings and a steam crane for moving large cargo. The excellent, child-friendly **Gloucester Waterways Museum ❹** (Llanthony Warehouse, The Docks; tel: 01452-318 200; http://canalriver trust.org.uk/gloucester-waterways-museum; daily 11am–4pm, July–Aug 10.30am–5pm; charge) has hands-on activities, interactive displays and video presentations, not to mention narrowboats and a steam dredger to explore. The museum tells the story of England's commercial waterways, from the canal-building mania of the late 18th century to their decline in the 20th century, brought about by the combined competition of road and rail transport. Exhibits cover ca-

Above: Gloucester's transformed docklands area provides an interesting contrast to the Old City.

nal construction, wildlife, cargoes and life on a narrow boat *(see box p.22)*. Moored beside the museum is *Queen Boadicea II*. You can board and take a 45-minute cruise through Gloucester Docks and along the Gloucester and Sharpness Canal; a commentary is included in the price of a ticket (tel: 01452-318 200; charge).

Another of the dockland museums concerns the more sober subject of warfare. **The Soldiers of Gloucestershire Museum ❸** (tel: 01452-522 682; www.glosters.org.

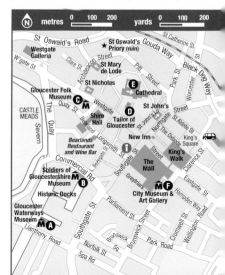

Ⓚ Gloucester for Children

The Gloucester Waterways Museum is particularly child-friendly and gives children an authentic and lively experience of waterways heritage. Children will love the hands-on, computer-based activities that really bring history to life: they can design their own canal boat, race boats and take them through locks, dress up as canal children, explore fabulous historic boats on the docks outside and go on a boat trip down the canal.

Above: paddle steamer afloat in Gloucester Docks.

uk; daily 10am–5pm, Jan–mid-Mar, Oct–Dec closed Sun; charge) covers the history of the Gloucestershire regiments from the late 17th century, with a reconstruction of a World War I trench and sections on women at war and Northern Ireland. Almost opposite this museum are the red-brick walls of Gloucester Gaol, which closed in 2013.

Shopping options at Gloucester Docks are impressive. Anchoring the south end is Gloucester Quays Shopping Outlet Centre, which can meet all expectations in discounted shop-

Above: the House of the Tailor of Gloucester in College Court.

ping. Inside a Victorian warehouse, the Antiques Centre (99a Orchard Street; tel: 01452-529 716; www.gacl. co.uk) houses 100 dealers over three floors and is one of the largest and oldest antique centres in the UK.

Westgate

Beyond the gaol, following signs to the centre, you should end up in Westgate Street – if not, you are unlikely to get lost, because the centre retains its Roman grid layout, with four main streets: Westgate, Northgate, Eastgate and Southgate street.

At the end of Westgate Street furthest from the centre is the **Gloucester Folk Museum** Ⓖ (99–103 Westgate Street; tel: 01452-396 868; www.livinggloucester.co.uk; Tue–Sat 10am–5pm; free). The museum occupies a fine timber-framed merchant's house built around 1500, now packed with a miscellaneous collection of objects from working model railways and a stuffed Gloucester Old Spot pig, to displays showing traditional methods of fishing for salmon and elvers in the River Severn. Newer extensions to the rear house a dairy and ironmongers shop, and the museum has a good programme of activities for children at weekends and during school holidays.

On the opposite side of Westgate Street, narrow lanes lead through to the cathedral close. One of these lanes – College Court – is lined with timber houses, including the **House of the Tailor of Gloucester**  (tel: 01452-422 856; www.tailor-of-gloucester.org.uk; Mon–Sat 10am–5pm, Sun noon–4pm; free). The famous story *The Tailor of Gloucester* by Beatrix Potter (1899–1943) was based on real people and events. The tailor was one John Prichard, who had been commissioned to make a waistcoat for the mayor of Gloucester. Having cut out the parts, he left his shop for the weekend and returned to find the waistcoat complete, with the exception of one buttonhole. A note pinned to the garment explained 'No more twist'. From that time on Prichard advertised his services with a sign saying: 'Come to Prichard where the waistcoats are made at night by fairies'. Years later, two of his assistants revealed that they had let themselves into the workshop and sewn up the waistcoat for a joke.

This shop in College Court is not the original tailor's premises, but is the one that Beatrix Potter used as the inspiration for the watercolours she painted to accompany her tale.

The Cathedral

On exiting the passageway of College Court, you emerge on College Green, with its wonderful view of **Gloucester Cathedral** (tel: 01452-528 095; www.gloucestercathedral.org.uk; daily 7.30am–after Evensong, parts may be closed for services; guided tours: Mon–Sat 10.30am–3.15pm, Sun noon–2.30pm; tower tours: Apr–Oct Wed–Fri 2.30pm, Sat 1.30 and 2.30pm; donation). This fine Norman church is relatively small by cathedral standards. The nave, with its massive columns, dates from Abbot Serlo's building campaign, which began in 1089 and ended in 1121. The other great building period began in the 14th century, after Edward II, murdered at Berkeley Castle in 1327, was brought to this church for burial. The combined income from the pilgrims who flocked to the late king's tomb, and the funds donated by successive

Below: Gloucester Cathedral's 15th-century tower with its four delicate pinnacles is 225ft (69 metres) high and a landmark in the city.

Ⓚ Film Location

Gloucester Cathedral's magnificent architecture, stained glass and royal tombs may be more suited to adult visitors, but children will be enthralled by the fact that the cloister was transformed into the corridors of Hogwarts for the filming of *Harry Potter and the Philosopher's Stone* (2001). Take the tour – while Harry may have moved on there are still glimpses of the magic if you know where to look.

Above: the 'Hogwarts' cloisters of *Harry Potter* film fame.

English monarchs in expiation of the regicide, funded the reconstruction of the cathedral's choir and transepts.

The marvellous east window, which fills the entire east wall of the nave, dates from this period, as do the choir stalls with their misericords (one of which is carved with an early representation of the game of football). Two tombs in the choir are not to be missed: the very fine wooden effigy of Robert, Duke of Normandy, William the Conqueror's eldest son, depicted in crusading armour on the southern side, and the shrine of Edward II himself, on the northern side, lying with his head supported by cherubs. Off the north aisle is Gloucester's chief claim to architectural innovation. The

ceiling of the cloister is beautifully decorated with fan vaulting – invented in Gloucester and later used in King's College Chapel and the Chapel Royal at Windsor.

City Centre

From the cathedral, follow Westgate Street into the centre of town where the two principal axes meet at the Cross. The original medieval cross has long gone, but there are several notable buildings nearby. At the crossroads itself is the 15th-century tower (all that survives) of St Michael's Church.

A short way up Northgate Street is **New Inn**, a rare surviving example of an enclosed courtyard inn, with tiers of open galleries. The inn was built in 1457 to accommodate pilgrims visiting Edward II's tomb. A short way up Southgate Street is a 1904 shopfront belonging to Baker the Jewellers. This is of interest primarily because of its fine figure clock. The elaborate timepiece features Father Time, John Bull, a kilted Scotsman and women in Irish and Welsh national dress, all holding the bells that strike the hours. Two doors up is the flamboyant Jacobean

Above: the tower of Gloucester Cathedral is just visible above College Court lane.

timber facade of the town house of the lords Berkeley (1650).

In Eastgate Street, remains of the Roman East Gate survive below modern street level and can be viewed through a glass superstructure let into the pavement. Just beyond, on the right, Brunswick Road leads to the **City Museum and Art Gallery** ❻ (tel: 01452-396 131; www.livinggloucester.co.uk; Tue–Sat 10am–5pm; free), where the various strands of Gloucester's history are drawn together. The star exhibits are nearly all archaeological. They include the outstanding 10th-century Saxon sculpture found during excavation of St Oswald's Priory, built by Aethelflaed, Queen of Mercia and daughter of Alfred the Great: and the intricately carved bone and ivory backgammon set, dating from the 1070s. Two exhibits in bronze were made more than 1,500 years apart: the Birdlip mirror is an outstanding example of pre-Roman Celtic design, with an intricate geometric pattern filled with enamel, while the closing ring made for St Nicholas' Church, Westgate, in 1300 is an extraordinary example of medieval metalworking, cast in the form of a man poking his tongue out and wearing a hood that takes the form of a horned and winged demon. Reopened in 2011, the museum has undergone a major makeover and as a result features a new café and improved permanent displays, such as a Roman kitchen, medieval street and the Story of Gloucester Through the Ages, that promise a much more interactive experience.

---

❸ Eating Out

Berkeley
Yurt Restaurant
Berkeley Castle; tel: 01453-511 209; May–Sept Sun–Wed 10am–5pm, Apr and Oct Sun only.
Eat inside an authentic Mongolian yurt. Cream teas and homemade cakes feature alongside light lunches and more substantial dishes such as venison casserole. £

Slimbridge
Tudor Arms
Shepherds Patch; tel: 01453-890 306; www.thetudorarms.co.uk; Mon–Sat 11am–11pm, Sun noon–10.30pm.
In a pretty waterside location, this family-run free house has a good reputation for delicious home-made dishes. ££

Frampton-on-Severn
Bell Inn
The Green; tel: 01452-740-346; www.thebellatframpton.co.uk; food served daily 11am–9pm.

Overlooking the village green, the Bell Inn offers seasonal menus and Sunday roasts, and special children's options. ££

Arlingham
The Old Passage Inn
Passage Road; tel: 01452-740 547; www.theoldpassage.com; Tue–Sat noon–2pm, 7–9.30pm, Sun noon–2.30pm.
On the banks of the River Severn, this acclaimed restaurant has a fabulous fish-based menu. £££

Gloucester
Bearlands Restaurant and Wine Bar
Bearlands House, Longsmith Street; tel: 01452-419 966; Tue–Sat noon–3pm, 7–11pm.
In a candlelit vaulted cellar dating back to 1740, you will find traditional and contemporary dishes on the menu, like pan-fried pigeon breast with pancetta and pot-roasted guinea fowl with merlot and root vegetable jus. £££

Tour 2

South Cotswolds

Skirting the edge of the Cotswolds, this full-day excursion is about 52 miles (84km) long and takes in the market town of Tetbury, stately manors and ancient sights

Tetbury, with its royal connections and individual shops, is a superb base for exploring the Cotswolds; located within easy reach of larger towns and cities such as Cheltenham and Bath). As the tour ventures beyond Tetbury, the ever-changing scenery is not always typical of the Cotswolds. Rural, narrow lanes take you off the beaten track to large expanses of unpopulated places, untouched by tourism, on occasion offering spectacular panoramic views. The route is littered with prehistoric sites and places to visit, including the National Arboretum and Woodchester Park. This is good walking country with several points from where you can pick up the Cotswold Way (see box p.53).

Highlights

- Tetbury
- Westonbirt, The National Arboretum
- Newark Park
- Uley
- Owlpen Manor
- Woodchester Park and Mansion

TETBURY

Our tour begins at **Tetbury ❶**, a quiet backwater until Prince Charles moved to Highgrove, on the southern outskirts of the town, delighting local estate agents who now describe property in the area as 'situated in Royal Gloucestershire'. Many of the 17th- and 18th-century town houses lining Long

F Woolsack Race

Branching off Market Place in the centre of Tetbury is Gumstool Hill, with its punishing 1 in 4 steep incline. Every spring bank holiday this is the site of the Woolsack Race when contestants run up and down the hill carrying a 66lb (30kg) bale of wool, a contest that probably started as a trial of strength between young farmers, designed to impress the local girls.

Above: encouraging the Woolsack Race contestants up a Tetbury hill.

Far Left: Chipping Steps, Tetbury.
Above: Long Street is lined with shops selling antiques and collectibles.

Tetbury's glory is its wonderfully theatrical **church**, a very rare example of Georgian Gothic, built in 1781 and with nearly all its furnishings intact. What has changed (as you can see from old photographs hung on the nave wall) is the position of the pulpit. If you stand where the pulpit once stood, you really do feel like an actor standing centre stage, with tiers of seating rising all around you.

Heading southwest out of Tetbury on the A433 Bath road, you pass Prince Charles' home, **Highgrove House**,

Street (Tetbury's main street) are now the premises of antiques dealers, so if you are interested in seeing what these houses look like inside you can always feign an interest in buying an old oak dresser or Georgian corner cupboard. No excuse is needed to gain admission to the **Tetbury Police Museum** (63 Long Street; tel: 01666-504 670; Mon–Fri 10am–3pm; free). It displays relics of Cotswold law enforcement in the old cells of the former police station and in the courtroom above.

In the centre of the town, the Market House, dating from 1655, is an elegant structure on stone pillars with space for an open market below and a covered market upstairs (Sat and Wed). Off to the left is Gumstool Hill, where each spring the Woolsack Races take place *(see box above)*.

Above: Westonbirt, The National Arboretum has a huge variety of mature trees and shrubs from temperate climates around the world.

on the right after about 2 miles (3km), though it is hidden behind high walls. Opposite is Doughton manor, an almost untouched 17th-century house with a fine barn, which probably dates from medieval times.

WESTONBIRT, THE NATIONAL ARBORETUM

Just 2 miles (3km) further on is **Westonbirt, The National Arboretum** ❷ (tel: 01666-880 220; www.weston birtarboretum.com; daily 10am–8pm or dusk if earlier; charge). This glorious estate was created in 1829 by the 21-year-old Robert Holford, who planted many of the fine trees that give the arboretum its structure. Interplanted among the trees are camellias, azaleas, rhododendrons, magnolias, cherries and maples. These beautiful shrubs and trees bring thousands to Westonbirt during spring and autumn. There is always something to see or an event taking place: the illuminated trail in December is particularly magical.

The arboretum represents only a small part of Robert Holford's estate. He also owned the village of **Weston-birt** on the opposite side of the road, and all the land surrounding his huge mansion (now the Westonbirt School for Girls). The stunning mansion and Italianate terraced gardens are occasionally open to the public (tel: 01666-881 373; www.holfordtrust.com). Failing that, go to the churchyard for a view of the gardens and the school, a flamboyant French-style neo-Baroque building designed in 1863 by Vulliamy. Holford has a magnificent mock-medieval tomb in the church.

DIDMARTON

Continuing southwest the next village of interest is **Didmarton**, which has a heartening story for those who love old churches. The 19th-century parishioners wanted a modern church, so they built a new one on a green-field site further up the Bath road, leaving the characterful medieval church unchanged. Today's parishioners have brought the old church back into use, returning all the furnishings, including the brass chandeliers and the altar table that had been removed to the Victorian building. Didmarton's church

Above: the Beaufort coat of arms on an estate house in Badminton.

is a treat, set opposite a spring known locally as St Lawrence's Holy Well, and stands adjacent to the 17th-century manor and tithe barn.

THE BADMINTONS

Continuing along the Bath road, you pass the Worcester Lodge entrance to **Badminton Park** ❸ on the left, an imposing domed Palladian structure designed by William Kent around 1746. This is all you will see of Badminton Park unless you happen to be here for the horse trials in May. However, you can drive through the estate; as the A433 merges onto the A46 take the immediate next left to Badminton. The route passes through **Little Badminton** and on to **Badminton**, with its imposing 18th-century estate houses. These are not low cottages, but terraces of nobly proportioned houses, with pediments carrying the Beaufort coat of arms, rendered and limewashed in pink and caramel. As proof of the architectural variety of the Georgian era, look out, as you drive through Badminton towards Acton Turville, for the *cottages*

ornés, with their deeply overhanging thatched roofs supported on rustic posts, and for farm buildings disguised as follies with Georgian Gothic windows and battlements.

THE SODBURYS

At the junction in the centre of Acton Turville, head west towards Chipping Sodbury. Cross over the junction with the A46 and continue through Old Sodbury and then turn right for **Little Sodbury**. The tour takes you through narrow country lanes that are right on the southern edge of the Cotswolds proper. Just before you reach Little Sodbury, turn right at the junction and a bit further on you can pull off the road and walk up a broad footpath to Little Sodbury hillfort, built in the Iron

Ⓢ Highgrove Inspiration

Among Tetbury's many delightful shops is a listed building housing the Highgrove Shop (10 Long Street; www.highgroveshop.com). This collection of organic foods and products for the home and garden has been inspired by Highgrove itself or reflects the interests and passions of HRH The Prince of Wales. Everything is unique and all profits from the sales are paid to the Prince's Charities Foundation.

Above: handmade Lebanese soap for sale in the Highgrove shop.

Above: today horses graze within the ancient perimeter ramparts of the Little Sodbury hillfort.

Age with massive double ramparts and commanding views that stretch westwards over the Forest of Dean and into Wales. Little Sodbury church is far less imposing, a humble structure built in 1659 from masonry taken from the demolished Little Chapel, behind Little Sodbury manor, where William Tyndale preached in the 1520s. It was here that he was first inspired to translate the Bible into English.

HIDDEN HAMLETS

As you leave Little Sodbury, turn right at the junction and then left following signs for Horton. About 2 miles (3km) further on turn right for Horton Court (not open to the public) with its 12th-century **Norman hall**, which belongs to the National Trust. Continue northwards to **Hawkesbury**. The road passes along the Cotswold Escarpment through unploughed sheep pasture, which bears the marks of ancient agriculture in the form of ditches, banks and terraces. Turn right for Hawkesbury itself, worth a visit just for the fine 15th-century church (often locked) with a monument to Lord Liverpool (1770–1828), prime minister at the time of the Battle of Waterloo (1815). Continue north past the church and turn right at the junction; soon you will pass a 100ft (30-metre) tower that looks like a cross between Cleopatra's Needle and a medieval lighthouse. Erected in 1846, the **Somerset Monument** commemorates General Lord Somerset, who served under Wellington at Waterloo. Sitting in the middle of nowhere on the top of a high hill it serves as a useful navigational aid for walkers. A few miles further on

Below: the village of Hawkesbury with its 15th-century church. Notice the ancient terraces of unploughed sheep pasture in the background.

Above: roses growing adjacent to Rose Hill School in Alderley.

at **Alderley**, the church, a pretty Georgian neo-Gothic structure, is now the chapel for the adjacent Rose Hill School; in the churchyard is the grave of the botanical artist Marianne North (1830–90), whose works are displayed at the Royal Botanic Gardens, Kew, in London.

FORGOTTEN VALLEYS

Beyond Alderley, a right turn signed to Ozleworth leads into one of several isolated valleys that make exploring the Cotswolds such an adventure. The road runs along Ozleworth Bottom to the gates of Ozleworth Park. A public footpath runs through the park grounds to **Ozleworth Church**, a curious Romanesque structure with a hexagonal central tower.

Continue uphill from Ozleworth and take the sharp left signposted to **Newark Park** ❹ (tel: 01793-817 666; Mar–Oct Wed–Sun 11am–5pm, with exceptions; charge). Newark (the name is a contraction of 'New Work') was built as a hunting lodge by Sir Nicholas Poyntz in 1540 using timber and masonry from the demolished Kingswood Abbey, near Wotton-under-Edge. James Wyatt remodelled the house in 1790, giving it neo-Gothic external details and Adam-style interiors. When leaving Newark Park turn left, then left again to continue to Wotton-under-Edge.

WOTTON-UNDER-EDGE

These lonely valleys are quite a contrast to the bustle of **Wotton-under-Edge** ❺, a former mill town with a heritage centre in the old fire station at **The Chipping** (tel: 01453-521 541; www.wottonheritage.com; Tue, Thu–Fri 10am–1pm, 2–4pm, Sat 10am–1pm, with exceptions). North of Wotton, along the B4060 towards Dursley, the escarpment becomes increasingly steep as you approach **North Nibley**, where there is a car park at the entrance to the village and a footpath up through beech woods to the Tyndale Monument on Nibley Knoll. William Tyndale was burned at the stake in 1536 for heresy – his crime was to translate the Bible from Latin into English, a revolutionary act condemned by a Catholic Church fearful that its authority would be undermined if people could read and interpret the Bible for themselves. Tyndale's labours were not entirely in vain, for large parts of his translation were incorporated into the Authorised King James Version of 1611. The **Tyndale Monument**

Above: Tyndale Monument can be reached up a path from North Nibley, and has great views from the top.

Above: view from the green in the former mill village of Uley, looking east in the direction of the hidden Owlpen Valley.

takes the form of a tower, 111ft (34 metres) high, which can be climbed for sweeping views. It was built in 1866 in the belief that Tyndale was born in North Nibley, but it is now thought he was born in the Welsh Marches.

Above: look out for the statue of Queen Anne at the eastern end of the market house at Dursley.

DURSLEY AND THE SECRET VALLEY

When you reach the junction with the A4135 turn right and continue on to the centre of **Dursley**. Just past the market house and town hall of 1738, with a statue of Queen Anne, take the B4066 east to **Uley** ❻. This former mill village was once famous for its blue cloth and for the militancy of its weavers, who formed illegal and secret trade societies (the forerunners of trades unions) to maintain the value of their wages. Lower down in the village are rows of weavers' cottages, while around the green are the houses of the mill owners and merchants. The church, though rebuilt in 1857 under the influence of the evangelical Oxford Movement, has some fine tea-caddy tombs in its churchyard.

OWLPEN MANOR

From Uley's green you can take a detour down a narrow road that heads east into the hidden Owlpen Valley, with the beautiful 15th-century **Owlpen Manor** ❼ (only open to the public for group bookings; tel:

Above: Owlpen Manor is a Tudor gem set in a lovely Cotswold valley.

01453-860 261). Dating back to at least 1464, the manor escaped improvements and stood empty between 1850 and 1926, when the Arts and Crafts architect Norman Jewson restored it with a lively appreciation for its beauty, antiquity and setting. Highlights include the Cotswold Arts and Crafts Movement furniture and the 17th-century painted cloth wall hangings in the bedroom. The early 18th-century gardens were described by Vita Sackville-West as 'a dream …

amongst dark secret rooms of yew, hiding in the valley'. There are lovely walks through the wooded valley to the other buildings of the estate (now converted to holiday accommodation), such as the 18th-century Grist Mill. Behind Owlpen Manor is the small but ornate Victorian church, decorated with mosaics, stained glass and encaustic tiles.

ANCIENT SIGHTS

Back in Uley, the steep road out of the village passes several important prehistoric monuments. First comes **Uley Bury** Iron Age hillfort, one of the most spectacularly sited in the Cotswolds, with extensive views from the summit. Less than a mile (1km) north is **Hetty Pegler's Tump ❽**, one of the best-preserved neolithic long barrows in the Cotswolds. Named after the person who owned the land in the 17th century, the tump was built around 3000 BC, and deliberately sited on this prominent hilltop so as to be visible from afar. There is another similar barrow (Nympsfield), with explanatory boards set up by English Heritage, just over 1 mile (1.5km) further on at the **Coaley Peak** picnic site *(see box below)*.

Ⓥ Coaley Peak Viewpoint

Coaley Peak is a popular spot for pulling off the road to picnic, fly a kite or take a leisurely stroll through the adjacent woodlands. But the most obvious attraction as you turn into the car park is the view, which on a clear day stretches panoramically over the River Severn to a backdrop of the Forest of Dean and the Welsh hills beyond. The Cotswold Way National Trail runs through the site.

Above: Coaley Peak provides one of the best views across the Severn Valley.

Above: fan vaulting and fine views at Woodchester Mansion, the neo-Gothic Victorian building left unfinished near Nympsfield.

WOODCHESTER PARK AND MANSION

Just past Coaley Peak, opposite is a turning for the entrance to **Woodchester Park** (daily 9am–dusk), set in another secret Cotswold valley and owned by the National Trust. There is a pay-and-display car park at the entrance to the park and from here you can walk for miles to observe the plants and wildlife. Badgers, buzzards and sparrow hawks inhabit the valley and a number of rare species of orchids grow here.

A third of the way down the 3-mile (5km) long valley sits **Woodchester Mansion** ❾ (tel: 01453-861 541; www.woodchestermansion.org. uk; late Mar–Oct 11am–5pm, check website for opening days; charge), which is a striking but unfinished 19th-century house begun in 1854. Based on a design by Pugin, the house is a fusion of French Gothic and traditional

ⓖ Protecting the Bats

The attic at Woodchester Mansion is set aside as a maternity roost for the endangered greater and lesser horseshoe bats, where breeding females take up residence in summer. 'Batcams' in the observatory allow visitors a closer look. In the late 1950s bats at Woodchester numbered around 400 but by 1986 only 85 survived. From 1994, a programme of sensitive management was introduced and the bat numbers steadily increased – in 2011 numbers had risen to over 1,000.

Above: endangered bat species roost in the attic at Woodchester Mansion.

Cotswold styles. Before the house was completed, the builders were taken off to work on another project. They left their tools behind, expecting to return, but never did. The house remains frozen in time, a bat- and owl-haunted spot *(see box, left)*.

BACK TO TETBURY

From Woodchester Park, go back to Tetbury via Nympsfield, then follow signs to Kingscote to join the A4135; turn left and follow the road back to Tetbury. It's worth stopping in **Beverston** on the way through to look at the church (behind the road on the left) with its weatherworn Saxon carving of the Risen Christ on the tower, and its fine 13th-century nave. Next door is 13th-century Beverston Castle. The building is privately owned but opens under the National Gardens Scheme on certain days in summer (tel: 01666-502 219; charge).

E Eating Out

Tetbury

Chef's Table
40 Long Street; tel : 01666-504 466; www.thechefstable.co.uk; Wed–Sat noon–2.30pm, 7–9.30pm, Mon–Tue noon–2.30pm.
The experienced chef/owner puts his classical training to good use in the first floor bistro's open kitchen. Dishes might include Salcombe crab thermidor, truffle and parmesan souf-flé or homemade pork faggots with parsnip purée. ££

Conservatory Restaurant
Calcot Manor, on the A4135 near Tetbury; tel: 01666-890 391; www.calcotmanor.co.uk; daily noon–2.15pm, 7–9.30pm.
For that special occasion – fine views, a chic candle-lit dining room and an impressive seasonal menu that uses locally produced organic meat and vegetables – the Conservatory is just the place. £££

The Two Toads
19 Church Street; tel: 01666-503 696; www.twotoads.co.uk; Mon–Sat 9am–5pm, Sun 10.30am–4.30pm.
Aside from the acclaimed traditional cream teas, this long-established tea shop also serves wholesome breakfasts, light lunches such as baguettes or jacket potatoes, and a mouth-watering selection of homemade cakes. You can eat in the pretty courtyard during warm weather. £

Old Sodbury

Dog Inn
Old Wood Lane; tel: 01454-312 006; www.the-dog-inn.co.uk; Mon–Sat 11am–11pm, Sun noon–3pm, 7–10.30pm.
This charming 500-year-old build-ing on the Cotswold Way offers an extensive menu, full to the brim with delicious home-cooked food, which is a welcome sight to the walkers that often drop in. Good-value lunch menu. £–££

Uley

The Old Crown Inn
tel: 01453-860 502; www.theold crownuley.co.uk; food served daily noon–2pm, 5–9pm, Sat–Sun all day in summer.
This quaint, white-bricked pub offers a wide variety of traditional pub fare from baguettes and pies to steak and fish, plus a range of local ales, includ-ing those from the local brewery. ££

Kingscote

Hunter's Hall Inn Restaurant
tel: 01453-860 393; www.huntershall inn.co.uk; daily 8am–10pm.
Ivy clad Hunter's Hall Inn has a wealth of old charm. Eat in the timbered restaurant or one of the bars enhanced by blackened beams, shooting prints and stone hearths. Traditional pub favourites. Large garden. ££

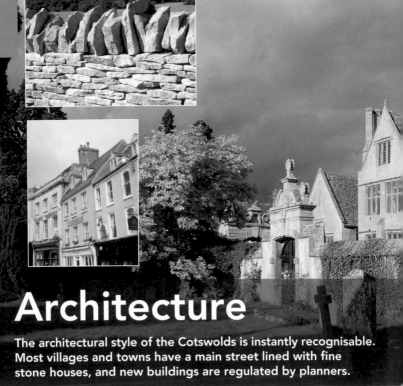

Architecture

The architectural style of the Cotswolds is instantly recognisable. Most villages and towns have a main street lined with fine stone houses, and new buildings are regulated by planners.

Nowhere else in England has quite such a recognisable style of architecture as the Cotswolds. Village after village has the same signature main street of beautiful stone houses, and strict planning regulations govern the design of new buildings.

COTSWOLD STYLE

The Cotswolds' architectural style is simple yet effective. Roofs are steeply pitched for the stone tiles that are applied in a fish-scale pattern down to the eaves. The eaves overhang the walls because, in the absence of guttering, this was the best way of carrying rainwater well away from the walls. Other features that look decorative but which are entirely practical do the same job of shedding water, especially the drip moulds found around the chimney stack and above windows and doors. Window frames are also made of stone. Some buildings have extra features – dormer windows or Italianate details such as round or lozenge-shaped windows or rusticated quoins and door and window surrounds.

The principal difference between the houses of the rich and the poor is that

comparatively recent phenomenon). The effect of adding colours to the lime wash resulted in a polychromatic look that had its own charm.

OLD CHURCHES AND NEW FASHIONS

There is a rich tradition of Saxon and Norman churches throughout the Cotswolds, which continued into the medieval period when many were built from the prosperity of the wool trade. The quality of the local stone enabled intricate carving to enhance the beauty of the buildings. Cotswold churches also have some unusual Romanesque features and Elkstone church (see p.57) is the outstanding example.

Canals brought new materials, such as brick, in the late 18th century and building styles changed – Cheltenham, for example, looks very different from most other Cotswold towns because it was largely constructed by speculative builders using pattern books based on what was in vogue in London at the time.

ARTS AND CRAFTS INFLUENCE

The Arts and Crafts Movement brought a reaction against the new styles, and those towns and villages where the movement was at its most active have some fine early 20th-century buildings that look as if they have been there for centuries. There were several different Arts and Crafts groups espousing the ethics of William Morris, fleeing from London like the great artist himself, to seek a refuge from urban ugliness and industrial values.

Following in Morris's footsteps were C.R. Ashbee, who set up the Guild of Handicrafts in Chipping Campden in 1902; and the Cotswold Arts and Crafts Movement, led by Ernest Gimson and the Barnsley brothers, established at about the same time.

grander buildings were constructed of cut-stone (known as ashlar), with mortar joints so narrow as to be almost invisible. Humbler buildings were made of rubble – stones of random size – cemented by thick beds of lime mortar. Rubble buildings were frequently lime washed to give them the same smooth appearance as their grander neighbours (the bare stone that characterises towns and villages today is a

Above: the Jacobean Stanway House.
Top Left: dry stone walls criss-cross the Cotswold hills. **Centre Left**: colourful facades and steeply pitched roofs in Cirencester. **Left**: a country church.

Tour 3

Stroud and the Mill Valleys

Centred round the market town of Stroud, this 42-mile (68km) drive through steep valleys and dales is half a day well spent uncovering the area's best-kept secrets

This tour offers a very different Cotswold experience from that of the landscape found in the heart of the area. The circular route begins and ends in the historic town of Stroud, which played an important role in the Industrial Revolution and is located at the divergence of five valleys. These gorge-like valleys, with their fast-running streams, provided the ideal conditions for woollen mills in the 18th century, when cloth production ceased to be a cottage industry and grew to become a factory-based process. As the drive weaves its way through the valleys, there are several pretty, hidden villages and hamlets en route, as well as elegant towns that display Cotswold stone houses at their best.

Highlights

- Stroud
- Nailsworth
- Minchinhampton
- Bisley
- Slad Valley
- Painswick and the Rococo Garden

STROUD

Once the centre of the industry in this area, **Stroud ❶** still has the feel of an industrial town. The centre of Stroud has been pedestrianised and there is an enviable array of specialist shops with a bohemian vibe to explore. The award-winning Farmers' Market is held every Saturday. History trail maps can be obtained from the Visitor Informaon Centre (tel: 01453-760 960) located in the Subscription Rooms on George Street, a handsome classical building dating from 1833, built as its name says by public subscription as a concert hall and art gallery. It still performs this role, especially during the annual Stroud Fringe Festival, held end August/September (www.stroudfringe.co.uk).

Also of interest is Stroud's **Museum in the Park** (tel: 01453-763 394; www.museuminthepark.org.uk; Apr–Sept Tue–Fri 10am–5pm, Sat–Sun 11am–5pm, Aug daily, Oct–Mar Tue–Fri 10am–4pm, Sat–Sun 11am–4pm; free). This family-friendly museum is set in a restored Georgian mansion in Stratford Park. Innovative displays feature local history and pride of place goes to the world's first lawn-mower, invented nearby in 1830.

Two of the town's surviving woollen mills are open to the public: Dunkirk Mill, where a working water wheel can be seen driving textile machinery; and St Mary's Mill (for both mills tel: 01453-766 273; www.stroud-textile.org.uk; days and times are restricted, call or check the website for details; charge).

THE NAILSWORTH VALLEY

From Stroud heading south on the A46 to Nailsworth, you pass Rooksmoor Mills (1820), Woodchester Mill and, finest of all, with its French-château-style clock tower, Ebley Mill (now home to Stroud District Council). The latter was built in 1818 and extended by G.F. Bodley, the church architect, in 1865.

In the vibrant little town of **Nailsworth ❷**, the mill theme continues, with the late 18th-century Clothiers Arms (tel: 01453-763 801) and mill-workers' cottages. Nonconformism came early to these valleys,

ⓖ Alternative Town

Stroud has led the way since 1990 as a thriving alternative centre proud of its green credentials. Shops selling organic food and sustainable goods are plentiful in the town. Ecoshop (Stroud Valleys Project) at 8 Threadneedle Street has eco-friendly products to help you live a sustainable life. Stroud also has Britain's first organic café, Woodruffs *(see p.47)*, while the nearby valleys are home to a growing community of artists and New Agers.

and Chestnut Hill has a fine Quaker Meeting House dating from 1689. At the bottom of the valley, Egypt Mill (now a hotel and restaurant) was a corn mill that was later used for cloth dyeing, while on the Old Bristol Road Ruskin Mill (tel: 01453-837 500) is now a college. It has a coffee shop serving organic food and an exhibition gallery showing the work of violin- and cabinet-makers, jewellers, sculptors and other artists.

Above Left: industrial heritage in Stroud. **Below**: clock tower and war memorial in Nailsworth town centre.

penned the immortal couplet: 'Wha is this life if, full of care, We have no time to stand and stare'. At the junction turn right for Amberley.

Amberley is where the Victorian novelist Maria Craik wrote much of her novel *John Halifax, Gentleman* (1856), setting chapters against the background of the local mills. Unfenced roads lead across the common, a popular spot for picnics, kite-flying and horse riding in summer. Parts of the common are rich in rare limestone wild flowers in summer, including harebells, rockroses, orchids and stemless thistles.

Above: Amberley is within easy reach of several other mill towns and has lovely views of the valleys.

From Nailsworth, very steep roads climb to the extensive limestone grasslands of Minchinhampton Common. Heading for Amberley, you will pass through the one-street hamlet of Watledge, the last home of W.H. Davies, who wrote about his wanderings in Britain and America in *Autobiography of a Super-tramp* (1908), and

Minchinhampton

Following signs for Minchinhampton, you pass the ditches and banks known as the Bulwarks, thought to have been defences thrown up in the 1st century AD by local Iron Age tribes to halt the advancing Romans.

Minchinhampton ❸ was another prosperous wool town, and the

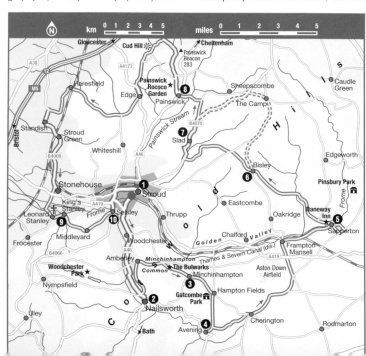

scores of ancient tracks that converge here were used by packhorses bringing wool for sale from nearby farms. The pillared Market Hall (1698) has survived, surrounded by fine 17th- and 18th-century houses. The church spire, oddly truncated, was in danger of collapsing so it was reduced in height in 1563 and given a stone coronet. The south transept is a triumph of the 14th-century Decorated style, with a lovely rose window and unusual stone scissor-bracing.

Avening

Heading southeast to Avening, the road skirts the boundary of **Gatcombe Park**, home of the Princess Royal. **Avening** ❹ was another village that prospered on the cottage-based industry of skilled spinners and weavers. The fine church, of Saxon origin, contains a monument to Henry Brydges (died 1615), who was a notorious pirate, smuggler and highwayman until he married the daughter of a prosperous Avening clothier.

Just before Avening turn east on a minor road. The next village, **Cher-**

Above: picturesque Avening once had a thriving cottage industry of spinners and weavers.

ington, has several more 18th-century clothiers' houses, distinguished buildings of stone with moulded eaves, architraves and cornices. From Cherington village centre turn left and take the next narrow lane signed Sapperton, skirting Aston Down airfield, a favourite spot for launching gliders, to descend into another valley system, where the route crosses the A419 to **Frampton Mansell**.

THE GOLDEN VALLEY

There are fine views from Frampton's neo-Norman church (1844) over the Golden Valley – in autumn the beech trees that clothe the valley's sides turn to gold. Frampton is a good spot to park for walking the Thames and Severn Canal Path in the valley bottom.

Canal Path Walk

The Thames and Severn Canal was built to link the River Severn with the River Thames (at Inglesham Lock). The canal's working life was short-lived because water continually leaked into the porous limestone, and in 1876 the Great Western Railway, whose track still runs parallel, bought the canal to prevent any rival company building another track along its course. Since

Above: cows graze on the plateau just above Frampton Mansell and the Golden Valley.

then the canal has been left to nature, and walking the towpath can be a challenge, but it will bring you close to moorhens, coots and grebes, dank lock basins alive with midges, sunny pools where dragon- and damselflies hunt for prey, and bogs fragrant with watermint or musk. Enjoy this natural wilderness while it lasts: the Thames and Severn Canal Restoration Trust has financial backing to restore the canal to full working order.

Take the narrow road downhill in front of the Crown Inn *(see p.47)* and cross the railway line to pick up the path. Heading west takes you past natural lakes formed by the River Frome, which runs alongside the canal for much of its length. At **Chalford** there are several historic mills grouped around the former wharf, as well as a canal roundhouse, once occupied by the lengthman, whose job it was to maintain a length of the canal. If you go east, you will pass the Daneway Inn *(see p.47)* before reaching the Sapperton end of the rock-cut canal tunnel, framed by an imposing classical portal. From here, boats would be propelled the 2½ miles (4km) through the tunnel to the Coates end by leggers, who lay on their backs and 'walked' along the tunnel walls.

Sapperton

The driving tour continues to **Sapperton ⑤**, built on a series of terraces overlooking the Golden Valley. There are several good walks from the village, including the woodland path to Pinbury Park, the home of the poet John Masefield, and the place where Ernest Barnsley, Sidney Barnsley and Ernest Gimson first set up their Cotswold Arts and Crafts furniture-making workshops. All three are buried in the churchyard at Sapperton. The church itself, rebuilt at the beginning of the reign of Queen Anne, has big round-headed windows and pews made from Jacobean carved woodwork, recycled when Sapperton House was demolished in 1730. Also of note are two fine Renaissance tombs, one to Sir Henry Poole (died 1616) and the other to Sir Robert Atkyns (died 1711), author of the first history of Gloucestershire, which he is holding. Retrace the route to the crossroads

Below: remnant of the industrial age at Chalford, where historic mills are grouped around the old wharf on the Thames and Severn Canal.

Above: outside the Daneway Inn below Sapperton.

and turn right, following signs to Bisley, about 3 miles (4.5km) further on.

At Daneway, in the valley below Sapperton, the steep hillside to the north of the **Daneway Inn** *(see p.47)* is covered in grassy tussocks indicating the presence of old ants' nests, characteristic of unimproved Cotswold grassland. These fields, known as the Daneway Banks, now form part of a Gloucestershire Wildlife Trust reserve where you can see several varieties of orchid in summer.

Bisley

A steep road runs northwest of the Banks and through beech woodland to the delightful village of **Bisley** ❻, where footpaths thread their way between dry stone walls sheltering colourful cottage gardens in the vicinity of the fine 15th-century church. Thomas Keble (brother of John Keble, the Oxford Movement founder, vicar here from 1827 until his death in 1875) introduced the annual well-dressing ceremony held on Ascension Day, based on the spring-fed stone tanks in the lane south of the church. The novelist Jilly Cooper lives in this village.

THE SLAD VALLEY

To reach the secluded Slad Valley *(see p.9)*, leave Bisley village northwest on Stroud Road to join Bisley Road and then take the very narrow lane on the right, signposted Catswood, about half a mile (1km) outside the village. Not much more than a track in places, the road twists and turns passing a disused quarry, now a Gloucestershire Wildlife Trust reserve with many species of orchid, adders, lizards, butterflies and rare grasshoppers. At the end turn right to pass through **Slad** ❼ *(see box below)* and take the next left signposted Painswick.

❻ Life in Slad

Poet and novelist Laurie Lee lived most of his life in the village of Slad and was best known for his autobiographical trilogy. The first volume was *Cider with Rosie* (1959) which depicts life in Slad at the end of World War I. An adaptation of Laurie Lee's story was televised by the BBC in 1970 and again in 1998 by the former Carlton Television. The story has since also been adapted for radio and the stage.

Above: the late writer Laurie Lee walking in the hills above Slad.

G The Large Blue

Extinct in the UK since 1979, the Large Blue butterfly has been successfully reintroduced at Royal Bank overlooking the Slad Valley, a region where it has not been seen for 50 years. It is believed that, due to climate change, the Cotswolds offers the best environment for the butterflies to thrive, with warmer conditions ideal for the red ants on which they rely for food at the caterpillar stage.

Above: the rare Large Blue butterfly can thrive in the Cotswolds.

If you prefer a less arduous route, just before the narrow lane, branch left on Stancombe Lane, following signs for The Camp, and continue to the junction with the B4070. Turn left and after about 2½ miles (4km) turn right to Painswick – you are now back on the same route.

THE PAINSWICK VALLEY

From Slad it is a short drive down a steep single-track road to **Painswick** ❽, often described as the 'Queen of the Cotswolds' because of its elegant and harmonious groups of classically inspired Cotswold stone houses. This, too, was a wool town, and the Painswick Brook, at the bottom of the valley, has several former fulling mills, now converted to apartments.

The magnificent churchyard is famous both for the 99 topiary yews, which form a series of avenues leading to the church, and for the unusual collection of tea-caddy and table tombs. These are mostly the work of 18th-century masons, and they are carved with all kinds of Baroque decorative devices, including cherubs, fruit and flower swags, pie-crust frills, scrolls and shells. The church contains a number of curiosities, including graffiti carved into a pillar in the north nave by an imprisoned Puritan soldier

during the 1643 siege of the village. It quotes from Edmund Spenser's *The Faerie Queene* – 'Be bolde, be bolde, be not too bold'. Painswick celebrates its ancient Clypping Ceremony on or around 19 September, when children from the parish link hands to form a circle right round the church (clipping derives from *clyppan*, meaning to embrace) while singing songs.

Britain's oldest Bowling Green (over 400 years old), is located at the back of the Falcon Inn in Painswick. The flat green, established in the 16th century, was originally used for gentlemen to

Above: the Woolpack in Slad, a welcoming 16th-century watering hole, once frequented by Laurie Lee.

Above: clear directions to amenities in elegant Painswick, a town often described as the 'Queen of the Cotswolds'.

wind down after a day of hunting in the nearby Cotswold countryside.

The Gardens

Drive through the centre of town and on the northern outskirts of Painswick, on the B4073 Gloucester road, is the entrance to the **Painswick Rococo Garden** (tel: 01452-813 204; www. rococogarden.co.uk; mid-Jan–Oct daily 11am–5pm; charge). A rare survivor from the early 18th century, it represents the transition in styles from the formal to the natural landscape schools of gardening. Dotted with temples and gazebos and a maze celebrating its 250th anniversary, the garden enjoys a naturally dramatic setting in a sheltered combe, with woodland on all sides. The garden is magical throughout the year, and is particularly breathtaking in late January/early February when snowdrops appear. The Coach House Restaurant serves lunches and tea.

Viewpoints

Bearing left on a concealed single-track road, soon after a sign for Painswick Beacon (see box opposite), will take you in a big loop via a viewpoint at Cud Hill. The narrow road eventually

meets the A4173. Head south and almost immediately take the next right, which works its way through more rural lanes, and eventually turn right again towards Haresfield. Here the

Ⓥ Painswick Beacon

Above the town of Painswick, just north of the Rococo Garden, this viewing point offers spectacular views right across the Severn valley and takes in the Welsh mountains in the distance. On the top of the beacon the outlines of a large Iron Age hillfort can be seen. The fort is triangular in shape and has double banks and ditches on three sides.

Above: view from the Cotswold scarp at Painswick Beacon.

Above: a rambler's view from the Cotswold Way over Selsley village and church to Stroud.

views to the south look over a patch-work of dairy farms and orchards to the silvery Severn, while to the north they stretch along the escarpment to Cheltenham and beyond. As the road descends into the flat vale you arrive at **Haresfield**, where the Tailor of Gloucester, John Prichard, lived later in life as a schoolmaster. The church has some good monuments inside and fine table tombs outside.

RETURNING TO STROUD

At the next junction turn right, then left (signed Gloucester), and left again for Standish. Standish Church, where the boldly carved skeletons and cherubs have escaped weather erosion, also has some good monuments and tombs. Inside there is a splendidly painted memorial to Sir Henry Winston, an ancestor of Sir Winston Churchill.

The Stanleys

Continue to **Stonehouse**, from where you cross the 18th-century Stroudwater Canal on the way to Leonard Stanley, where the parish church once served the monks of the Augustinian priory of St Leonard, founded in 1121. The fine Roman-

esque capitals of the chancel depict the Nativity and Mary Magdalene drying the feet of Jesus with her hair. The original parish church (of Saxon origin) still survives in use as a cart shed in the adjacent farmyard, along with a 14th-century monastic barn and fishpond (they can be seen from the western end of the churchyard).

The tour continues south to **King's Stanley** ❾. Straddling the River Frome, the magnificent Stanley Mill has been restored with funding from English Heritage. It's a pioneering example of fireproof construction: iron and brick were the main materials used

Below: detail from one of the splendid Arts and Crafts stained-glass windows in Selsley Church.

when it was built in 1815, and wood was banned altogether.

Selsley Church

Further south from King's Stanley, left at a mini roundabout, a narrow road climbs through Middleyard to **Selsley** ❿ and one of the Cotswolds' most delightful Victorian churches. The church and the adjacent house were built by Sir Samuel Marling, owner of Ebley Mill, whose French-style clock tower is visible in the valley as you look to the right across the churchyard. Marling had once visited the village of Marlengo in the Austrian Tyrol, because of its similarity to his own name. He decided Selsley was sufficiently alpine in feel to justify the construction of a church based on that at Marlengo; the result is this striking building designed by the architect G.F. Bodley in 1862. The stained glass here was the first to be designed by the then newly formed firm of Morris & Co. William Morris, Philip Webb, Ford Madox Brown, Dante Gabriel Rossetti and Edward Burne-Jones all had a hand in the design of the lively and colourful Creation window that fills the west gable. From Selsley it is just a short drive back to the centre of Stroud.

Ⓔ Eating Out

Stroud
Woodruffs Organic Café
24 High Street; tel: 01453-759 195; www.woodruffsorganiccafe.co.uk; Mon–Sat 8.30am–5pm.
For health-conscious eaters, this organic café is an excellent spot for afternoon tea or a full-on lunch. £–££

Nailsworth
Egypt Mill Hotel and Restaurant
Stroud Road; tel: 01453-833 449; www.egyptmill.com; daily 10am–9.30pm.
In a lovely riverside setting, the restaurant has wooden floors, birdcages dangling from the ceiling and a working mill on show. The menu intertwines great British ingredients with food from across the world. ££

Frampton Mansell
The Crown Inn
Frampton Mansell; tel: 01285-760 601; www.thecrowninn-cotswolds.co.uk; food served Mon–Sat noon–2.30pm, 6–9.30pm, Sun noon–8.30pm.
A quintessential village pub in a 17th-century cider house, with open fires, stone interiors, a friendly environment and refined pub grub. Fine views. ££

Sapperton
Daneway Inn
Daneway; tel: 01285-760 297; http://thedaneway.com; daily 11am–2.30pm, 6.30–11pm, closed Mon eve.
Hearty dishes such as beef and Guinness pie are huge crowd pleasers at this charming pub with original features and a large garden edging the now derelict canal. ££

Bisley
The Bear
George Street; tel: 01452-770 265; www.bisleybear.co.uk; food served Mon–Sat noon–2pm, 6–9pm, Sun noon–3pm.
The epitome of a 16th-century inn: oak settles, brass and copper, stone fireplace, and low ceiling. Tasty meals can be enjoyed outside on the flag-stoned courtyard. £–££

Painswick
JK's @ St Michael's
Victoria Street; tel: 01452-813 832; www.jks-restaurantco.uk; Wed–Sun noon–3pm, 7–10pm.
In a 17th-century listed building, this cosy restaurant run by two local chefs who support local farms offers modern cuisine with a twist. £££

Tour 4

Cirencester to the Churn Valley

After a morning's sightseeing in Cirencester, this 42-mile (68km) circular drive, over hilltops and through valleys, conjures up the feeling of being miles from anywhere

As you leave the walled town of Cirencester, the contrast ahead quickly becomes apparent as the tour winds through hamlets invisible to anyone from the main road and along lanes framed by perfect arches of overhanging trees. The valleys rise and fall, offering some stunning views, and there are grand architectural gems, beautiful gardens and country parks hidden among the lush countryside. The road back to Cirencester dips in and out of yet more peaceful settlements featuring some fine churches.

CIRENCESTER

A glance at a map reveals that **Cirencester ❶** sits at the hub of a

Highlights

- Cirencester
- Duntisbourne Abbots
- Miserden
- Prinknash Abbey and the Bird and Deer Park
- Crickley Hill Country Park
- Elkstone
- Cerney House Gardens

network of Roman roads – the Fosse Way, the Ermin Way, Akeman Street, the White Way – and that Cirencester itself retains the rectilinear street plan of a Roman town. Founded in

Left: the parish church of St John the Baptist, with its imposing tower, stands on Cirencester marketplace.
Above: the Corinium Museum.

idence of their daily lives, including an audio-visual display, which brings you face to face with the residents. One of the museum's most impressive objects is a Roman column capital, intricately sculpted on all four sides with Bacchic figures and sitting atop a 16ft (5m)-high replica column. The Anglo-Saxon Gallery reveals treasures from the cemetery site of Butlers Field, Lechlade. The museum also covers the English Civil War and the story of the Cotswolds woollen industry.

Turning left out of the museum will take you up Black Jack Street, past the Edwardian tiled shop front of Jesse Smith the butcher *(see box, below)*, to the church of St John the Baptist, with its magnificent tower and two-storey fan-vaulted porch opening onto the broad and handsome marketplace (market held on Monday and Friday).

Inside the church, the riches range from the precious Anne Boleyn cup (1535) and the lovely 15th-century wine-glass pulpit to numerous fine funerary monuments and brasses and the wall paintings and fan-vaulting of St Catherine's Chapel. If the tower is open at the time of your visit, it is worth climbing to the top for a view of Cirencester Mansion, built by the

the 1st century AD as Corinium Dobunorum, it was the second largest city in Roman Britain, exceeded in size only by London.

The museum and the church

Gardeners in Cirencester are used to turning up Roman pottery and fragments of mosaic, and any building project must be preceded by an archaeological investigation, the fruits of which are displayed in the excellent **Corinium Museum** (tel: 01285-655 611; www.coriniummuseum.cotswold.gov.uk; Apr–Oct Mon–Sat 10am–5pm, Sun 2–5pm, Nov–Mar until 4pm; charge) in Park Street. The museum contains a remarkable collection illustrating more than 12,000 years of Cotswold life. Here you can experience the Roman town of Corinium through reconstructions of the forum basilica complex, and rooms from a wealthy Roman town house, as well as the museum's spectacular mosaics. The mezzanine floor focuses on the people of the town and the ev-

Ⓢ Butcher in Black Street

If you miss the twice weekly Cirencester market, don't worry, just head for Jesse Smith's, the butcher in ancient Black Jack Street, which has won numerous awards for its sausages, raised pies and meat from rare breed livestock. In what was the old pheasant-plucking room around the corner in The Stableyard is Jesse Smith's Cheese Shop, which offers a mouthwatering array of fresh cheeses and olives.

ⓢ New Brewery Arts

In the heart of Cirecester, housed in a converted brewery (1820), New Brewery Arts is one of the best centres of contemporary craft in southern England. There are resident craft workers on site specialising in glass-blowing, hand-printed textiles, clothing and ceramics. The superb Main Gallery holds exhibitions of local artists' work and there is a craft shop and coffee house (www.newbreweryarts.org.uk).

first Earl Bathurst from 1714 to 1718, and hidden from view at street level by the world's tallest yew hedge.

Cirencester Park

Beyond the mansion are the broad tree-lined avenues of the 30,000-acre (12,150-hectare) **Cirencester Park**. This is an early example of English landscape gardening, laid out by Bathurst with the aid of his friend, the poet Alexander Pope. The walk to the park entrance passes through several of Cirencester's most handsome streets: Dollar Street, Coxwell Street, Thomas Street and Cecily Hill, all lined by houses of 17th- and 18th-century wool merchants. Shopping can be a delight in Cirencester, as the town has a variety of speciality shops among the courtyards and the many historic streets that radiate from the town centre *(see box)*.

THE DUNT VALLEY

Whichever way you journey out of Cirencester, you quickly get into fine countryside. Heading north on the A435, just after you pass through Stratton, turn west to reach the deep tree-

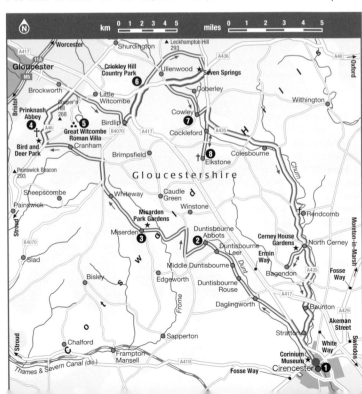

Above: headstones line the path leading to the church at Duntisbourne Abbots.

shaded lanes of the Dunt Valley, stopping first at **Daglingworth,** where the church has some unusually well-preserved Saxon carvings of the Crucifixion. Most of the churches around Cirencester are of late Saxon origin (10th century) but many have been re-built several times over as architectural fashions changed. Continue to follow signs to the Duntisbournes (you will need to venture off this road to visit the centre of these villages). One that retains much of its original appearance is the tiny church at **Duntisbourne Rouse**, where the nave is Saxon, the chancel early Norman and the saddle-backed tower is 15th-century.

Heading on through Middle Duntisbourne and Duntisbourne Leer, there are several idyllic farmsteads to be seen if you divert off to the right to the bottom of the valley. In each case the farm buildings are grouped around the river, which forms a ford. Between Duntisbourne Leer and Duntisbourne Abbots the river actually flows down the main road for a distance of some 30yds/m, deliberately diverted in this way to create a water lane to wash the clay off the wheels of carts and the fetlocks of horses as they re-

turned from the fields. For most of the year, the water is too deep for cars to negotiate, but walkers can follow the raised stone-flagged footpath that runs alongside.

The church at **Duntisbourne Abbots** ❷ sits at the centre of the village on a plateau surrounded by stone cottages built on terraces cut into the hillside. Eighteenth-century tombs carved with cherubs and skulls line the churchyard path and the door retains its original 15th-century iron-work and closing ring.

THE UPPER FROME VALLEY

From the Dunt Valley, head westwards to the lovely wooded valley of the upper Frome, following signs to Sapperton and Winstone. At the junction turn right and just before you reach Winstone, turn west towards **Miserden** ❸ and take the turning into the centre of the village. The church here is Saxon, and the south aisle contains two outstanding monuments. One is topped by a painted stone effigy of William Kingston (died 1614), with a

Below: old stone walls and cottages hug the hillside in delightful Duntisbourne Abbots.

Right: the tranquil walled garden at Prinknash Abbey.

Right: the tranquil walled garden at Prinknash Abbey.

wonderfully naturalistic heraldic goat at his feet, chewing on the branch of a tree. The other, crisply carved in alabaster with careful attention to every lacy detail of the clothing, depicts Sir William Sandys (died 1640), his wife, Margaret Culpeper, who died four years later, and their large family. A more humble tomb in the churchyard, on the right of the path as you leave the church, has a brass plaque that well illustrates the lost art of epitaph composition. It marks the grave of a shepherd named Samuel Horrel, who died in 1807, and reads:

From youth through life the sheep was all his care
And harmless as the flock his manners were
On earth he held the faith to Christians given
In hope to join the fold of Christ in heaven

Manicured Miserden is an estate village, and the big house lies at the opposite end from the church, sign-

Above: Michaelmas daisies in bloom.

posted **Misarden Park Gardens** (tel: 01285-821 303; www.misarden park.co.uk; Apr–Sept Tue–Thur 10am–4.30pm; charge). The house (not open to the public) is Elizabethan in origin, built by the Sandys family and extended with a Renaissance-style loggia and east wing by Sir Edwin Lutyens. The gardens are set on a series of terraces with extensive southward views down the beech-clad Frome valley. The outline of the garden, with a central walk lined by ancient yew hedges clipped into dome-shaped battlements, dates from the 17th century. The walled garden contains fine displays of roses and clematis, while the lower terraces are planted more informally with flowering trees and shrubs, and masses of naturalised bulbs.

The road through Miserden loops around the village to rejoin the original route you were on; continue north, passing through **Whiteway**. This unusual hamlet of single-storey timber houses was built by the ancestors of the present occupants who came here as early pioneers of self-sufficiency – not in the 1960s as you might expect, but in 1898, inspired by

the ideas of the Russian novelist and Christian mystic, Count Leo Tolstoy.

At the next junction turn right and then right again to join the B4070. The next left will take you to **Cranham**, where the church has a pair of sheep shears carved among the gargoyles on the splendid tower.

PRINKNASH ABBEY

Turn left at the junction, then right, to join the A46 and to visit **Prinknash Abbey** ❹ (pronounced 'Prinage'; tel: 01452-812455; www.prinknashabbey. org.uk; gift shop and tea room daily 10am–4pm), where another group of self-sufficient Christians settled among the glorious beech woods three decades later, in 1928. The Catholic Benedictines who founded the monastery took over a 16th-century house that had once belonged to the abbots of Gloucester, and they began extending it in 1939, using stone and wood quarried and felled on the site.

To pay for the work, the monks founded a pottery where they created the distinctive black-lustre glazed ceramics that were to become their trademark. The pottery has since closed, but incense and rosaries made

by the monks can still be purchased from the shop.

The pottery now houses the remarkable reconstruction of the Great

ⓖ The Cotswold Way

This long-distance walk starts at Chipping Campden, winding its way through beautiful countryside for 102 miles (164km) before concluding in the city of Bath. You can pick up part of the trail at various places along the route, or take a holiday walking the entire Cotswold Way, staying at some lovely spots en route (www.nationaltrail.co.uk).

Above: all Cotswold Way signage will have the acorn symbol.

ⓕ Cheese Rolling

The 2010 Cooper's Hill cheese-rolling contest was officially cancelled amid concerns for safety. But that didn't stop loyal competitors taking to the hill and thousands of spectators showing up to create their own versions of this world-famous event. All the competitors made it down the hill in one piece with only minor injuries. The historic event has continued to grow in popularity since then but who knows what the future holds?

Above: helter-skelter down Cooper's Hill in pursuit of cheese.

Orpheus Roman Pavement. The original mosaic villa floor, dating from c.AD325, is buried beneath a churchyard in nearby Woodchester. The new abbey, completed in 1972, is a distinctive modern building.

In the monastic grounds, run as a separate enterprise, is the **Bird and Deer Park** (tel: 01452-812 727; www.thebirdpark.com; Mar–Oct daily 10am–5pm, Nov–Feb until 4pm; charge). Here, set among woodland, is a series of ponds, bridges and islands where waterfowl, tame fallow deer, African pygmy goats and large carp, will try to persuade you to feed them.

Below: Great Witcombe Roman Villa, in a delightful sheltered setting.

Miniature donkeys Toffee and Treacle are popular with children. Plans for a new Visitor Centre are underway.

GREAT WITCOMBE VILLA

Continuing downhill on the A46 from Prinknash Abbey, it takes no time at all to descend from the glorious beech woods to the built-up outskirts of Gloucester. At the first roundabout, follow signs for the Witcombes and you will pass **Great Witcombe Roman Villa** ❺ (daylight hours; free) on the right. The villa enjoys a lovely setting, sheltered by the escarpment to the east, but with open views to the west. The villa remains consist of living rooms and bathhouses, plus some mosaics and hypocausts (underfloor heating systems) that are locked inside timber sheds. If you are here in summer, it is worth exploring the footpaths around the villa, for the wet meadows support many wild flowers, including drifts of orchids and ragged robin.

From the villa you can also see Cooper's Hill, to the west, the site of the traditional cheese-rolling contest held every spring bank holiday. This may have begun as a ceremony to stake out grazing rights, and it involves chasing a Double Gloucester cheese, protected by a disk-shaped wooden case, as it rolls at speed down a steep grassy slope. This is no sport for the fainthearted (few contenders stay on their feet) and there have been attempts to ban it on grounds of safety, but the first to catch the cheese gets to take it home *(see box opposite)*.

COUNTRY PARKS

If you are keen on seeking out rare wild flowers, or if you just want to enjoy a walk along the breezy tops of the Cotswold escarpment, you can choose from the two country parks in the vicinity. Barrow Wake Viewpoint is reached by turning right (signed Birdlip) and heading up steep Birdlip Hill itself. At the top turn left onto the B4070. Several barrows (the heaps of earth that mark prehistoric tombs) dot the short-cropped grass on this hill, including the barrow from which the Birdlip mirror was excavated. Wild flowers to be found here include wild thyme and milkwort, pyramidal orchids and various vetches that attract small blue and brown butterflies.

A little further along the scarp is **Crickley Hill Country Park** ❻ (tel: 01452-863 170; daily 9am–5pm; free, charge for parking). At the junction, turn left onto the A417 and at the roundabout take the second exit following signs for the country park. The visitor centre (Apr–Sept 1.30–4.30pm, times erractic so check) here has displays charting the history of the Iron Age hillfort that occupies the western edge of the hill. Six way-marked trails with coloured posts are designed to explore the different areas of historical and geographical interest; a guide map is available from the visitor centre. This is one of several good spots from which to pick up the Cotswold Way if you want to walk just a part of its 102-mile (164km) length. There are hard-to-beat views over Gloucester and beyond to the Black Mountains in Wales – a viewing platform helps visitors to identify the various landmarks.

Fossil hunting at **Leckhampton Hill**, further up on the eastern side of the same road, has unfortunately reached nuisance proportions, and

Below: Barrow Wake Viewpoint on the Cotswold Way.

Above: Cowley Manor is now a luxury hotel, but the church behind can be visited via the main entrance.

there is scarcely an exposed rock face that has not been defaced by pointless and destructive hammering. There are several exposures here, showing the various oolitic beds that make up the Cotswolds, from the top layer of ragstone (used since Celtic times as a walling and house-building material) to the deeper layers of freestone (used from the 17th century onwards for smooth-fronted classical buildings). In fact, Leckhampton Hill served as the main quarry for the Greek-Revival buildings of Cheltenham (see p.37), the town that lies in the plain below. Following the main path through Crickley Hill Country Park you will find a prominent column of rock left by late 18th-century quarrymen, known as the Devil's Chimney.

CHURN VALLEY

Turn left out of Crickley Hill Country Park and take the second on the right, Hartley Lane (concealed entrance). After about 1½ miles (2.5km) this twisty lane joins the A 435/436 at the **Seven Springs** roundabout. Turn right to find the actual springs,

on the right-hand side of the A436 just after the junction. Here, clear spring waters bubble out from beneath a shelf of rock at several different points, forming the source of the River Churn. Some believe this is the true source of the Thames: certainly the Churn is considerably longer than its rivals for the title, from its source to the point where it meets the Thames at Cricklade. For that reason alone Seven Springs ought to be considered the fount of England's longest river. Instead, that honour goes to a rather dreary patch of dried-up mud, known officially as Thames Head, near Kemble, about 4 miles (6.5km) south of Cirencester. Continue for a further 2 miles (3km) and take the left turning signposted Cowley.

VILLAGES AND CHURCHES

The delightful River Churn contributes to the charm of the villages it passes through. At **Coberley**, which diverts to the left, the river forms a marsh that is bright with marsh marigolds, yellow flags, watermint and purple loosestrife, depending on the season.

The church, invisible from the road, is reached by pushing open a doorway in an ancient barn and crossing a farmyard. Inside are 13th- and 14th-century monuments to knights, clad in chain mail, and one to the mother of mayor of London, Dick Whittington.

At **Cowley ❼**, the river is dammed to form a series of cascades and a fish-filled lake fronting **Cowley Manor**. This handsome mid-19th-century building, in the Italian style, was built for Sir James Horlick, co-inventor of the famous bedtime beverage. The gardens have been replanted with drifts of naturalised bulbs and perennials by a well-known local garden designer, Noel Kingsbury. The manor has been converted into a luxury hotel. If staying here is not an option, you can still glimpse the gardens if you visit the small church in the grounds.

Follow the lane northeast around the hotel grounds to pick up the A435 and continue south back to Cirencester. It is worth detouring east and west of the A435 to explore the villages with their celebrated churches that line this stretch of road.

Above: entrance to Elkstone church, with stylised heads of beasts.

After about half a mile take the fork west to **Elkstone ❽**, where the quirky church is an outstanding example of the unusual Romanesque features that appear on some Cotswold churches. The heads of beasts form a guard around the south doorway, designed to keep demons at bay, and there is a tympanum showing Christ seated in majesty.

🄵 Romanesque Features

Some Cotswold churches have unusual Romanesque features. Scholars have plotted their distribution and come up with various explanations for their origin. A number of these features came to the Cotswolds from France and Spain by way of the pilgrimage route to Santiago de Compostela in northwest Spain. Medieval pilgrims came back full of enthusiasm for the Romanesque churches they had seen along the route and asked local Cotswold masons to produce something similar. The masons, it seems, were happy to oblige.

Above: Romanesque church doorway, Guiting Power (see p.93).

Inside are bold chevroned arches and dragon-head stops, and (uniquely) a pigeon loft above the chancel, reached via a stairway near the pulpit.

About 5 miles (8km) further south on the A435, to the east, **Rendcomb's church** is like Fairford's *(see p.100)* in miniature scale, sharing such features as an exceptionally fine and complete wooden chancel screen and some good stained glass, both dating from the early decades of the 16th century. The link is that John Tame built Fairford Church, while his son, Sir Edmund Tame, built the one at Rendcomb; it is likely that the same craftsmen worked on both churches. Rendcomb also has an outstanding Romanesque stone font, carved with figures representing 11 of the Apostles; the space for Judas is left blank. The church doubles as a chapel for the next-door school, which occupies another handsome Italianate house dating from the mid-19th century.

North Cerney to Baunton

A short way down the valley to the east, **North Cerney** church is packed with interest. On the outside are two large pieces of graffiti, perhaps doodled in an idle moment by the masons who restored the Norman church after a fire in the 15th century. One shows a leopard and another a mythological manticore (with the head of a man and the body of a beast), similar to drawings found in popular bestiaries of the period. Inside is a lovely rood screen supporting a figure of Christ carved in Italy c.1600, reminding us of how many parish churches would have looked before the iconoclasts of the Reformation period removed these features.

Up the hill from the church, **Cerney House Gardens** (tel: 01285-831300; www.cerneygardens.com; Jan–Oct daily 10am–5pm; charge) has spring bulbs in abundance, a working kitchen and herb garden and a splendid walled garden full of herbaceous plants and roses. Award-winning Cerney cheese, produced on the estate since 1983, is sold in the garden shop.

Across the A435 is **Bagendon**, surrounded by earthworks marking the boundary of the principal settlement of the Dobunni, the Iron-Age tribe after

Below: Bagendon's pretty church has Saxon origins.

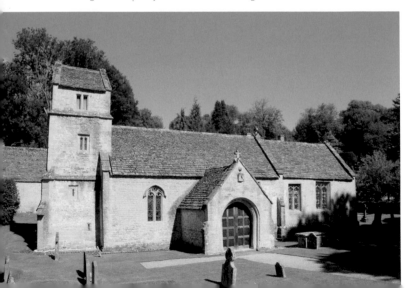

Right: sheep grazing in the meadows near Bagendon.

whom Roman Cirencester (Corinium Dobunorum) was named. From being the capital of a thriving Celtic community, with a mint and a metal-working industry, Bagendon has become a quiet backwater with a pretty Saxon church and Norman saddleback tower containing a priest's chamber.

One last church is worth a call: **Baunton** has a huge 14th-century St Christopher on the north wall. Fabulous fish swim around his feet, a ship rides at anchor in one corner, while a fisherman sits on one bank and a hermit stands by a chapel on the other.

Ⓔ Eating Out

Cirencester
Jack's Café
44 Black Jack Street; tel: 01285-640 888; Mon–Sat 9am–5pm, Sun 11am–5pm.
Typical English tearoom concealed in a small alleyway and always busy, offering divine home-made cakes, lunches, and a nice line in tea and coffee. £
Jesse's Bistro
The Stableyard, 14 Black Jack Street, tel: 01285-641 497; www.jesses bistro.co.uk; Mon–Sat noon–2.30pm, 7–9.30pm (closed Mon evening).
Fine local produce prepared with imagination, plus excellent service. Everything is cooked in the wood-burning oven, producing a unique flavour. ££–£££

Miserden
The Carpenters Arms
Stroud, tel: 01285-821 283; Mon–Sat 11.30am–3pm, 6–11pm, Sun noon–10.30pm, with exceptions.
A charming pub with an unspoiled interior in the idyllic village of Miserden. Blackboard menus display home-baked country fare using local suppliers. £–££

Cranham
The Black Horse
Cranham; tel: 01452-812 217; www.theblackhorsecranham.co.uk; Tue–Sun noon–2pm, 6.30–11pm.
Freshly made food includes sausage and bacon toad-in-the-hole and fisherman's pie. In summer you may find Morris men dancing. ££

Cowley
Green Dragon Inn
Cockleford; tel. 01242-870 271; www.green-dragon-inn.co.uk; Mon–Sat 11am–11pm, Sun noon–10.30pm.
This 17th-century inn is as pretty as a picture. Log fires, beamed ceilings and flagged floors set the scene for pub grub with a modern twist, and real ales. ££

North Cerney
The Bathurst Arms
tel: 01285-831 281; www.bathurst arms.com; food served Mon–Sat noon–2pm, 6–9pm, Sun noon–3pm, 7–9pm.
Beside the River Churn with a pretty garden that is used in summer for occasional barbecues. ££

Conservation

Conserving natural habitats, farmland, trees, traditional stone edifices and characterful buildings is of paramount importance in the Cotswolds

Despite the ruggedness of its scenery, the beauty of the Cotswolds is very fragile. What looks like a timeless landscape is, in fact, changing all the time.

EVER-CHANGING LANDSCAPE

In the Middle Ages, the Cotswolds consisted of unenclosed downland, providing uninterrupted grazing for sheep. In the 14th century, whole villages were depopulated to make way for sheep. A classic example is the deserted village of Upton, cleared in 1384 by the bishops of Worcester, though the house platforms and streets remain clearly visible as earthworks.

Another significant change occurred after 1750 when these open sheep walks began to be enclosed. It was at this time that many of the stone walls were built. Since 1945 the ploughing of pasture to create arable fields has changed the appearance of the Cotswolds yet again. Small fields have been merged to create larger ones by grubbing out hedges or removing walls.

Changes in farming methods have left many fine barns and farm build-

funds to encourage traditional low-intensity farming. Just about every town and village centre of note in the Cotswolds is now a Conservation Area, which means development is kept to a minimum. Where new dwellings are permitted, they have to conform to strict design criteria, using recycled Cotswold stone, lime mortar and wood-framed windows. Permission is now rarely given to convert barns to dwellings, although they may be used for small-scale industrial activities.

With an area as distinctive as the Cotswolds, the local authorities tread a tightrope. On the one hand they must maintain the life of the area and provide employment and housing; on the other, they have to try and preserve the essential character that attracts tourism and makes the Cotswolds such a desirable place to live. This has been achieved by allowing towns such as Cirencester *(see p.48)* and Stroud *(see p.38)* to develop while conserving others, such as Northleach *(see p.96)*, Stow-on-the-Wold *(see p.90)* and Chipping Campden *(see p.79)*.

THE FUTURE

The Cotswolds Conservation Board exists to protect the Area of Outstanding Natural Beauty and works with a wide range of partner organisations to ensure that this is achieved. Its plan until 2015 is to concentrate on key areas. These include climate change and its effects on the environment and wildlife; sustainable tourism; and encouraging local products for local markets. They also want to raise further awareness of the Cotswolds and promote outdoor activities to a wider, more urban audience.

ings redundant. Some have been converted into dwellings with mock Georgian front doors, introducing suburban values to the countryside. Where farmers have been refused permission to develop, they have left farm buildings to rot, often robbing them of masonry and stone roofing tiles.

HOLDING BACK THE CHANGES

A belated attempt has been made to harness this tide of change. The Cotswolds is now officially an Area of Outstanding Natural Beauty, a designation that theoretically restricts development and provides government

Above: a wild Cotswold meadow. **Top Left**: lunch by the River Eye. **Centre Left**: development has led to increased traffic. **Left**: waymark on the Cotswold Way.

Tour 5

Cheltenham and the Cotswold Escarpment

Taking in some of the best the Cotswolds can offer, you can extend this 18-mile (29km) drive to a full-day 34-mile (55km) tour with visits to Evesham and Tewkesbury

Starting your tour early in Cheltenham gives you the chance to shop in comfort and see the sights of this exceptional spa town before it gets too crowded. The journey to Broadway is a delight, with superb countryside, picture-postcard villages and grandiose buildings. From Broadway you can extend your drive or take bus 559 to Evesham and on to Tewkesbury (bus 540 from Evesham) in the western reaches of the Cotswolds region.

CHELTENHAM
Cheltenham ❶ town's coat of arms features pigeons because it was these

Highlights
- Cheltenham
- Winchcombe
- Sudeley Castle
- Stanway House
- Stanton
- Snowshill Manor
- Broadway
- Tewkesbury Abbey

birds, pecking at salt grains in a meadow outside the town, that led to the discovery of the mineral springs that were to make the town famous. The

Left: an elegant Regency terrace.
Above: the Neptune Fountain on Cheltenham's Promenade.

springs were discovered in 1716, but it was not until George II visited the town in 1788 that high society began to adopt Cheltenham as a summer resort.

In the three decades following the royal visit, the population increased seven-fold and £5 million was invested in speculative development. Row upon row of Regency houses, with fine wrought-iron balconies and fanlights, were erected around the Pittville Pump Room, with its graceful dome and pillared portico modelled on the temple of Illisus in Athens.

The focus of Cheltenham has shifted somewhat since the 18th century, and most visitors now arrive in the commercial heart, leaving their cars in one of the car parks that lie near the pedestrianised High Street. To rediscover Regency Cheltenham, head for the Promenade, or the Prom, as it is known locally. Noble Greek-Revival terraces line one side of this broad leafy avenue, where fortunes were once gambled away in smart gentlemen's clubs. Opposite are the tempting plate-glass windows of smart shops and the Cavendish

House department store. Neptune, god of the sea, dominates the splendid fountain at the upper end of the Prom, and nearby is a statue of Cheltenham-born Edward Wilson, one of the explorers who died on Scott's ill-fated Antarctic expedition of 1912.

If you continue up the Promenade, you will pass the elegant **Town Hall** on the left (now a major concert and festival venue) surrounded by the colourful Imperial Gardens, full of bright flowers. The luxurious Queen's hotel (see p.126) closes the vista as you look across the manicured lawns of the gardens. On the opposite side of the road is elegant Montpellier Walk (1825), with female caryatids (inspired by those of the Acropolis in Athens) and a fascinating mix of antique shops, delicatessens, designer boutiques and pavement cafés. Coming back down Montpellier Street, one block to the west, you will pass Cheltenham Ladies College, the renowned educational establishment founded in 1854.

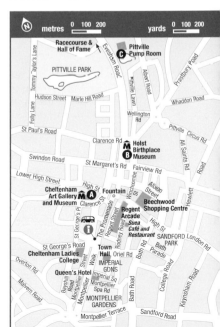

Above: statue of composer Gustav Holst, who was born in Cheltenham, in the Imperial Gardens.

Museums and Galleries

Passing along Royal Well Road and the stucco-fronted terraces of Royal Crescent, you will find, in Clarence Street, the excellent **Cheltenham Art Gallery and Museum Ⓐ** (tel: 01242-237 431; www.cheltenhammuseum. org.uk; daily 9.30am–5.15pm; free, charge for some exhibitions). The museum is packed with material on the history of Cheltenham and its people. Reopened in October 2013, the museum has undergone a £6 million development. The stylish new adjoining building houses the extensive fine art collection, local heroes' gallery, a gallery devoted to the Arts and Crafts movement, temporary exhibition space, Cheltenham Tourist Information, a café/bistro and a shop. The original building will continue to display local history, archaeology and unusual objects from Asia and Africa collected by local people.

Behind the museum, footpaths lead between grey tombstones past the parish church, one of Cheltenham's few pre-18th-century buildings, hidden behind the shops of the High Street. Turn right down the High Street, then fourth left, up Winchcombe Street. Continue north over Albion Street and Fairview Road, turning left into Clarence Road, to find the **Holst Birthplace Museum Ⓑ** (tel:

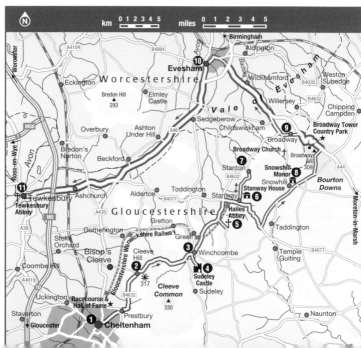

01242-524 846; www.holstmuseum.
org.uk; July–Sept Tue–Sat 10am–5pm,
Sun 1.30–5pm, Feb–June, Oct–mid-
Dec Tue–Sat 10am–4pm; charge),
the modest house in which composer
Gustav Holst spent the early part of
his life. Furnished in late Victorian
style, the house tells us as much about
life at the turn of the 20th century as
about Holst himself, composer of the
ever-popular *Planets Suite*.

Taking the Waters
From this point walk or drive up Evesham Road (about ½ mile/1km) to
the **Pittville Pump Room** ❻ (tel:
0844-576 2210; Wed–Sun 10am–4pm
but call in advance, times can vary;
free), set amid the manicured lawns of
Pittville Park. The Pump Room can be
closed at any time for functions but it
is still possible to take the waters. Under the Pump Room's dome, you can
sample the heavily mineralised water
that brought fame to Cheltenham. It
tastes so salty that you will only want
one sip, but it is said to be good for
constipation, rheumatism and gout,
among other bodily disorders. The
Pump Room plays host to regular
concerts and entertainment.

Above: a boutique in Cheltenham's
fashionable Montpellier district.

Cheltenham remains very much a
fashionable shopping centre *(see box,
left)* and is noted for its annual festivals
of jazz (May), science (June), classical
music (July) and literature (October);
the latter has been held for over 60
years (www.cheltenhamfestivals.com).
There is also a popular folk festival
held every February (tel: 01242-775
893). The town is never more festive
than during March, when members
of the racing fraternity descend on
the town for the Cheltenham Gold
Cup and the Champion Hurdle, the
premier events of the National Hunt
Festival. Taking the B4632 Broadway
road out of the town, **Cheltenham
Racecourse** is at Prestbury, some
2 miles (3km) north of the town; if
you cannot spend a day at the races,
you can always visit The Hall of Fame
(tel: 01242-513 014; times vary, check
in advance; free) and learn about the
history of the sport.

THE COTSWOLD
ESCARPMENT
Beyond Prestbury the B4632 climbs
the Cotswold Escarpment to reach

Above: not a typical golden Cotswolds town: Winchcombe's long main street is lined with buildings of various styles.

Cleeve Hill ②, where halfway up car parks allow you to pull off the road and walk up to the trig point on the summit. Here you are 1,040ft (317 metres) above sea level, and the views on a clear day take in every range of hills for 30 miles (50km) westwards. The highest point in the Cotswolds, at 1,080ft (330 metres), lies 2 miles (3km) south on Cleeve Common, but at only 43ft (13 metres) higher, it is probably not worth the walk.

Below: exploring Hailes Abbey with an audio guide. The abbey was reduced to ruins in the Dissolution.

Winchcombe

Descending Cleeve Hill, you will soon reach the lovely town of **Winchcombe ③**, with its long main street and a church noted for its splendidly grotesque gargoyles. Inside the church are two stone tombs, claimed to be those of King Kenelf and his son, the boy martyr St Kenelm, said to have been murdered by his sister in AD 819 because of his fervent devotion to Christianity. The story was invented by monks at Winchcombe's Benedictine Abbey (of which no trace now remains above ground), but it drew plenty of pilgrims to the town and made the abbey one of the wealthiest in England in the Middle Ages.

Sudeley Castle

Just beyond the church, a lane leads off to the right to **Sudeley Castle ④** (tel: 01242-602 308; www.sudeley castle.co.uk; late Mar–Oct daily 10.30am–5pm; charge). The present

Above: the castle has a terrific super-size adventure playground.

castle dates from the 15th century, although it was deliberately ruined by Parliamentary forces during the Civil War. Left to decay for two centuries, it was made habitable again between 1837 and 1936.

The castle's most famous resident was Catherine Parr (1512–48), the sixth wife of Henry VIII. Six weeks after becoming a widow, Catherine married Sudeley's owner, the Lord

Above: Sudeley Castle.

Admiral Seymour, and moved to the castle here, though she only survived the king by a year: after giving birth to her only daughter, Mary, she died of puerperal fever, and was buried in Sudeley's chapel. During the Civil War, her original monument was lost, but there is now a fine alabaster tomb in the chapel, carved in 1859 with a serene effigy of the queen.

Surrounding the chapel are the romantic gardens first laid out by Emma Dent, who came to Sudeley on her marriage in 1852 and set about restoring the castle and its grounds. An indefatigable collector, she succeeded in furnishing the castle with an outstanding collection of Tudor and Carolean furnishings, paintings (including works by Parmigiano, Van Dyck and Rubens) and relics of the Civil War.

If you take children to Sudeley, you may have difficulty dragging them away from the big adventure playground in the grounds. The offer of a ride on a steam train on the **Gloucestershire Warwickshire Railway** (tel: 01242-621 405; www.gwsr.com; Apr–Sept most days (not Mon), Mar, Oct–Nov Sat–Sun, Dec Santa specials; charge; telephone for a timetable or see the website) might do the trick. This restored Great Western Railway line was extended in 2010 and runs between Laverton (6 miles/10km northeast of Winchcombe), Winchcombe, Toddington, Gotherington Halt (an ideal stopping-off point for walkers to explore the nearby hills) and Cheltenham Racecourse, a 20-mile (32km) round trip that includes the Greet tunnel. You can pick up the train at any of these stations.

Hailes Abbey
You might catch sight of trains chuffing along the line as you head for **Hailes Abbey** ❺ (tel: 01242-602 398;

www.english-heritage.org.uk/hailes; daily July–Aug 10am–6pm, Apr–June, Sept–Oct 10am–5pm, Oct 10am–4pm; charge), 2 miles (3km) northeast of Winchcombe, just off the B4632. Owned by the National Trust and managed by English Heritage, the Cistercian abbey was founded in 1246 by King John's son, Richard, the Earl of Cornwall. During the Dissolution the monastery was plundered for building materials. Little remains now except for footings. There is, however, an excellent museum containing finds from excavations that indicate how splendid the abbey once was.

Stanway and Stanton

Two miles (3km) north of Hailes is Stanway, reached by turning east off the B4362 onto the B4077. At this point you are greeted by a Jacobean gatehouse leading to **Stanway House** ❻ (tel: 01386-584 469; www.stanwayfountain.co.uk; house and fountain: June–Aug Tue and Thu 2–5pm, fountain plays 2.45–3.15pm and 4–4.30pm; watermill most Thursdays throughout the year; charge – joint or separate fountain-only tickets available). Even if the house is not

open, you can get a flavour of it from the churchyard. A majestic 14th-century tithe barn stands to the north of the church, while the house stands to the west. The house retains the feel of a 17th-century courthouse, with its period furnishings and family portraits. Pleasing gardens surround the house, complete with a splendid 18th-century water garden, with a formal canal, stone cascade and eight ponds. The restored watermill produces wholemeal flour from wheat grown on the Stanway Estate.

The centrepiece of the canal is the magnificent fountain, opened in 2004, that sends a single jet of water soaring 300ft (90 metres) into the air. As you explore the bedrooms at Stanway, think of the author James Barrie, who was a frequent visitor in the 1920s. Moonlight flickering across his bedroom wall is said to have inspired him with the idea of the fairy Tinkerbell in *Peter Pan*.

Carry on to **Stanton** ❼, an almost too perfect village of thatched stone cottages that have been beautifully maintained over the decades following the example set by the squire of Stanton Court in the early 20th cen-

❺ Dramatic Locations

Stanway House has been a popular venue for period dramas and films, among them the sumptuous production of William Thackeray's *Vanity Fair* (2004) starring Reese Witherspoon, and *The Libertine* (2007) starring Johnny Depp. The TV adaptation of Jane Austen's *Emma* (1996) was located at Stanway, as well as at nearby Sudeley Castle. Some of the scenes of the BBC series *Father Brown* (2013) were filmed in the grounds of the castle, as well as in Winchombe.

Above: the wonderfully exuberant gatehouse to Stanway House.

Above: inside the restored church at Stanton.

tury. Saddened by the loss of so many young men of the village in World War I, he also paid for the church to be restored by Sir Ninian Comper as a war memorial.

SNOWSHILL MANOR

Retrace your route to Stanway and take the B4077 Stow-in-the-Wold road for approximately 2 miles (3km) north for Snowshill. Follow signs for Snowshill, going through the village to **Snowshill Manor ❽** (tel: 01386-852 410; www.nationaltrust.org. uk; admission by timed ticket only, Easter–Oct Wed–Sun, and bank holidays, manor: noon–5pm, shop, restaurant and gardens: 11am–5.30pm; charge). The manor is the creation of the eccentric Charles Paget Wade, who devoted many years of his solitary life (1919–51) to restoring the handsome 15th- to 18th-century house and creating one of Gloucestershire's finest gardens. The Arts and Crafts influence in Wade's work is evident in the exposed timber roofs, the Tudor-style oak panelling

carved by Wade himself using period tools, and the magpie collection of objects that fill the rooms. These are all treasured examples of skilled craftsmanship, from samurai armour to musical instruments, clocks and locally made weaving- and spinning machines. The gardens, which were conceived by Wade as a series of outdoor rooms, form a delightful maze around the old manor house.

William Morris, the ultimate progenitor of the Arts and Crafts ethic, used to spend holidays not far from here in the Broadway Tower, set high on the Cotswold Escarpment, some 3 miles (5km) northeast of Snowshill.

BROADWAY

To reach the tower return to Snowshill village and take the first left-hand turn signposted to Chipping Campden and Bourton-on-the-Water. Turn left at the crossroads signposted Broadway Tower (2 miles/3km) and Chipping Campden and then left at Snowshill Lavender Farm. Turn left again, following the signs directing you to

Above: Arts and Crafts embellishment on the facade of Snowshill Manor, where Charles Wade lived.

Ⓕ Garden Architecture

Allied to the Arts and Crafts Movement was the Cotswold 'school' of gardening, whose leading lights included Charles Wade at Snowshill Manor, Mark Fenwick at Abbotswood and Lawrence Johnston at Hidcote. They owe their architectural style (with garden rooms defined by yew hedges and steps, pools and gazebos forming important focal components) to the influence of Edwardian architects such as Sir Edwin Lutyens.

Above: an outhouse at Snowshill, the woodwork painted in 'Wade Blue'.

Broadway Tower Country Park (tel: 01386-852 390; www.broadwaytower.co.uk; daily 10.30am–5pm (weather permitting); charge). Today the tower stands at the centre of the park, which is known for its red deer.

Broadway Tower Country Park also has a stylish new teashop *(see p.73)*, gift shop and picnic area and playground. The tower was built in the late 18th century by the Earl of Coventry and on clear days enjoys views over 13 counties from the roof platform. Even if it is too hazy to see that far, the tower is well worth visit-

Below: the sign outside the historic Lygon Arms Hotel.

ing for its exhibitions covering the history of the tower and the work and life of William Morris himself.

Broadway Village

The descent from Broadway Tower, via the steep road into **Broadway** ❾, provides a dramatic introduction to this manicured village, with its boutiques and art galleries, tea shops, restaurants and shopping mall. Fine buildings also line both sides of the village street, including the imposing Lygon Arms Hotel, a 16th-century building restored and run by the father of the renowned Broadway furniture-maker Gordon Russell in the early 20th century. Russell's workshops were a major employer in the village for many years. Located in the original workshop is the **Gordon Russell Museum** (15 Russell Square; tel: 01386-854 695; www.gordonrussellmuseum. org; Tue–Sun Mar–Oct 11am–5pm, Nov–Feb 11am–4pm; charge), which celebrates the work of Sir Gordon and his influence on the Arts and Crafts Movement, as well as the use of machines to bring well-designed furniture to a larger market. Broadway's church, not to be missed, lies

EVESHAM

The drive to Broadway provides plenty of attractions along the route but those who wish to venture further through this delightful area should take the A44 from Broadway to **Evesham** 🔟. The town lies in the famous horticultural Vale of Evesham and stands on the banks of the River Avon. The area around the river and the abbey is particularly pleasant. Visit the **Almonry Heritage Centre** (Abbey Gate; tel: 01386-446 944; www.almonryevesham.org; Mon–Sat 10am–5pm, Mar–Oct also Sun 2–5pm; charge), which also houses the visitor information centre, to learn about the history of the town including the bloody Battle of Evesham of 1265, and the fierce exchange of 1645 during the English Civil War. Close to the

Above: Broadway village street is lined by some fine buildings.

a good mile (1.5km) out of town to the south, next to the Jacobean Court House, whose ancient and bulbous yew trees spill over from the garden into the churchyard. The peaceful church, with its uneven tiled floor and rustic memorials, was left standing alone once a new church was built in Broadway in 1839, and as a result it feels like a place where time has almost stood still ever since.

Below: Broadway Tower dominates its surroundings and has views over 13 counties on a clear day.

Ⓖ Vale of Evesham

A fertile area in southern Worcestershire, the Vale of Evesham is the fruit and vegetable basket of England, sheltering beneath the Cotswold Escarpment. Particularly popular is asparagus, celebrated in an annual festival from the end of April until late June. Evesham plums and apples produce exceptional blossom, and three specially devised walks and a cycle ride (route maps available from the Visitor Information Centre in Evesham) take in the best of the blooms.

Above: the fertile Vale of Evesham yields bumper fruit crops.

Above: medieval buildings in Tewkesbury.

heritage centre, in the **Abbey Park**, are the remains of Evesham Abbey, demolished in the Dissolution of the Monasteries in 1536 to 1540. Fortunately the handsome Bell Tower remains, close to the two churches of All Saints and St Lawrence. There are pleasant walks through the park down to the river, from where you can take a boat trip along the River Avon.

TEWKESBURY

From Evesham take the A46 southwest to the charming town of Tewkesbury ⑪, following signs for the town centre. It retains one of the finest medieval townscapes in England with exceptional buildings and a labyrinth of narrow alleys and courts, and is host to Europe's largest medieval festival, which takes place on the second weekend of July on the site of the great Battle of Tewkesbury of 1471. Of particular interest in the town is the magnificent **Abbey** (tel: 01684-850 959; www.tewkesbury abbey.org.uk; Mon–Sat 8.30am–5.30pm, Sun 7.30am–6pm; free, but donation requested), on which work started in 1102, with the building consecrated in 1121. Museums include the **Town Museum** (64 Barton Street; tel: 01684-292 901; www.tewekesbury musuem.org; Mar–Aug Tue–Fri 1–4pm, Sat 11am–4pm, Sept–Dec Tue–Fri

⑦ Evesham Country Park

Just north of Evesham, this excellent country park has plenty to offer the whole family. The Evesham Light Railway runs at weekends and during the school holidays with a ride through the park and the chance to stop and walk by the river. There is also a farm shop, restaurant and a café, a courtyard with a diverse range of shops and a garden centre. Fun summer holiday activities for children are on offer, as well as seasonal craft fairs.

Above: family fun aboard the park's 15-in gauge miniature steam train.

noon–3pm, Sat 11am–3pm, Jan–Mar Sat only, check times; charge), which gives a good introduction to the history and community of Tewkesbury; and the **John Moore Museum** (41–2 Church Street; tel: 01684-297 174; www.john mooremuseum.org; Apr–Oct Tue–Sat 10am–1pm, 2–5pm, Nov–Mar Sat only, check times; charge) devoted to natural history and the countryside, plus a lovely cottage garden. The town attracts many visitors for its antique and speciality shops and for its twice-weekly market held on Wednesdays and Saturdays. The visitor information and heritage centre, with its Out of the Hat interactive exhibition, can be found at 100 Church Street (tel: 01684-855 040; Apr–Oct Mon–Sat 10am–5pm, Nov–Apr Mon–Tue, Fri–Sat 10am–4pm).

Tewkesbury made headlines in 2007 when devastating floods completely cut off the town under some 3ft (1 metre) of water. Many people were made homeless and lives were lost. There are indicators showing the level of the waters, in some places to near shoulder height. Precautions and flood defences have since been implemented but Tewkesbury remains vunerable, with further floods affecting the town in 2012 and 2013.

Ⓔ Eating Out

Cheltenham
Svea Café and Restaurant
24 Rodney Road; tel: 01242-238 134; www.sveacafe.co.uk; Tue–Wed 11am–3pm, Thu–Sat 11am–3pm, 6–11pm.
Svea offers a slice of Swedish hospitality just off the High Street. Classic and contemporary Swedish dishes. Perfect for coffee and cakes. £–££

Winchcombe
5 North Street
5 North Street; tel: 01242-604 566; www.5northstreetrestaurant.co.uk; Tue 7–9pm, Wed–Sat noon–1.30pm, 7–9pm, Sun noon–1.30pm.
This tiny, Michelin-starred restaurant offers some of the best food served in Gloucestershire. Local produce abounds in dishes such as chump of local lamb or breast of quail. £££

Broadway
Morris and Brown
@ Broadway Tower
Middle Hill; tel: 01386-852 945; www.morrisandbrown.co.uk; daily 10am–5pm.
Set in an old stone building, the interior is modern and airy with fine views over the park. Choose from paninis, fresh soups or more substantial mains. Outdoor seating, too. £

Tisanes
21 The Green; tel: 01386-853 296; www.tisanes-tearooms.co.uk; daily 10am–5pm.
A gorgeous little tearoom in a 17th-century Cotswold-stone shop. Excellent service, delicious cakes and wonderful teas and coffees. £

Evesham
Word of Mouth
19–20 Vine Street; tel: 01386-422 259, www.wordofmouthcafe.co.uk; Mon–Sat 9am–4pm.
All special dietary needs are catered for with the freshest of produce straight from the Vale of Evesham. Home-made breads and soups, local apple juice and much more. £

Tewkesbury
Owens Restaurant
73 Church Street; tel: 01684-292 703; www.eatowens.co.uk; Tue–Sat noon–2.30pm, 6pm–late, Sun noon–3pm.
Although housed in a beautiful 15th-century building, the menu is contemporary. Local produce used in season, such as partridge and venison. Express lunch menu available. £–££.

Tour 6

Towns and Gardens around the North Cotswolds

Starting at Stratford-upon-Avon on the northern edge of the Cotswolds, this 25-mile (40km) tour gives the perfect balance between town and country

It's best to start your tour early in Stratford, giving you a chance to miss the crowds that flock to Shakespeare's birthplace in their millions every year. There is so much to see in the town that you will appreciate the relaxing drive out into the country for the rest of the tour. If impressive gardens and scenic countryside are your thing, this tour will not disappoint you, and with visits to several delightful small towns in the North Cotswolds the picture is complete.

Above: the Royal Shakespeare Theatre viewed from across the river at Stratford-upon-Avon.

Highlights

- Shakespeare's Stratford
- Hidcote Manor Garden
- Kiftsgate Court
- Chipping Campden
- Blockley
- Sezincote
- Batsford Arboretum
- Moreton-in-Marsh

STRATFORD-UPON-AVON

Synonymous with Shakespeare, historic **Stratford-upon-Avon ❶** is crammed with memorabilia of the great bard. With some 3.5 million visitors

ⓖ On Your Bike

Five miles (8km) of disused railway line make the Stratford Greenway the environmentally friendly way of getting out and about. There are picnic sites on route, plus a café at Stratford Bike Hire *(see p.113 for details)* and at the mid-point of the route, Milcote. Child seats and infant trailers are available. There are also other itineraries including the Shakespeare Houses Tour. More routes can be downloaded on the council website (www.stratford.gov.uk/transport) or from the cycling charity Sustrans (www.sustrans.org.uk).

Above: Stratford Greenway follows a section of the old Honeybourne Line.

speare.org.uk; daily July–Aug 9am–6pm, Apr–Sept 9am–5pm, Oct–Mar 10am–4pm; charge, ticket includes entry to New Place, Hall's Croft and Shakespeare's grave, see p.76–77). Here too is the Shakespeare Centre, giving information on the bard from his birth in the house in 1564. To explore the rest of town turn left out of the house to the end of Henley Street and right into High Street.

Harvard House

Halfway down High Street is **Harvard House ❸** (tel: 01789-204 507; Tue–Sat 10.30am–4.30pm; charge), a beautiful timber-framed building dating from 1596. The link with Harvard College in the US dates from 1605 and the marriage in Stratford in that year of Katherine, daughter of Thomas Rogers, the builder of Harvard House, and Robert Harvard of Southwark. It was their son, John, born in 1607, who emigrated to America in 1637. On his death a year later he left half his estate as well as his library to help found a college in Cambridge, Massachusetts, renamed Harvard

to the town each year, it can get very crowded. However, there are escapes with walking and cycling trails *(see box, above)*, and opportunities to take a relaxing river trip. There are also several high-quality independent shops, an excellent farmers' market (Rother Street, first and third Saturday of the month), a weekly market (Rother Street, Friday) and some first class restaurants. For culture, the famous Royal Shakepeare Company's theatres are essential.

Shakespeare's Birthplace

To put the relationship of Shakespeare and his home town into context start your day in Henley Street at **Shakespeare's Birthplace ❶** (tel: 01789-204 016; www.shake

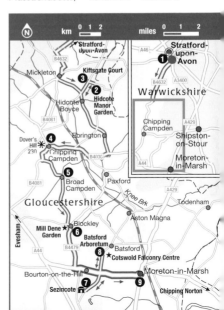

Above: Nash's House with the traditional knot garden in the foreground, Stratford-upon-Avon.

College by an order of 1639. The Stratford building is also the premises for the Museum of British Pewter.

Falstaff Experience

Take a detour left into Sheep Street to the award-winning museum, the **Falstaff Experience** 🄲 (40 Sheep Street; tel: 01789-298 070; www.fal staffexperience.co.uk; daily 10.30am–

> ### 🄺 Witches and Wizards
>
> For all fans of anything magical and creepy visit the Creaky Cauldron (www.seekthemagic.org) in Henley Street, Stratford. In the old-world 'shoppe' you can buy magic spells, wands, charms and much more. Enter if you dare the Enchanted Manor for time-travel, wizardry, myth and fairytale. You can take a break at the Golden Broomstick Coffee Shop. Theatrical perform-ances are staged in the evening with resident company Jadis Shadows, or you can join the Ghost Hunters for a paranormal experience.

5.30pm; charge), which is set in a magnificent Tudor building. Be trans-ported back to the 16th century, see a play at the theatre or join an evening ghost tour.

Nash's House and New Place

Return to Sheep Street and turn left into Chapel Street. The Shakespeare family home from 1597 and where Shakespeare died in 1616, **New Place** (Chapel Street; tel: 01789-204 016; www.shakespeare.org.uk; daily Apr–Sept 10am–5pm; Oct–Mar 11am–4pm; charge) is reached via **Nash's House** 🄳. The Elizabethan knot garden is well worth visiting. Between 2010 and 2012, excavations of the site revealed finds that are displayed in the 'Dig for Shakespeare' exhibition.

Hall's Croft

Continue into Church Street and turn left into Old Town. Shakespeare's daughter Susannah and son-in-law lived in **Hall's Croft** (tel: 01789-204 016; www.shakespeare.org.uk; daily Apr–Sept 10am–5pm; Oct–Mar 11am–4pm; charge). Here you can

Above: winter view of Holy Trinity Church, Stratford-upon-Avon.

see authentically furnished rooms and a lovely Elizabethan garden.

If you wish to visit Holy Trinity Church (open daily; free) and see Shakespeare's grave (small charge), continue along Old Town. For further attractions turn left along Southern Lane and head north, close to the river. For brass rubbing enthusiasts there is free admission to the Stratford Centre on the right or you can continue along to the theatres.

Royal Shakespeare Company

One of the best-known theatre companies in the world has three main venues in Stratford: the **RSC theatre** , the Swan and the Courtyard theatres (www.rsc.org.uk). Book tickets well in advance (0844-800 1100). Free performances can be seen at The Dell open-air theatre throughout June, July and August. You can enjoy walks beyond the theatres in the Bancroft Gardens or take boat trips from here.

Butterfly Farm

About five minutes' walk east from the riverside over Tramway Bridge is the

Butterfly Farm, Swan's Nest Lane; tel: 01789-299 288; www.butterfly farm.co.uk; daily 10am–6pm, till dusk in winter; charge), the largest in the UK. There are lots of creepy crawlies to see as well, including snails, crabs and spiders.

AROUND STRATFORD

There are several other Shakespeare-related attractions within a short distance of the town. You can reach **Anne Hathaway's Cottage** (Cottage Lane; tel: 01789-204 016; www. shakespeare.org.uk; daily Apr–Sept 9am–5pm, Oct–Mar 10am–4pm; charge) by driving or taking a footpath (1 mile/1.5km) off Evesham Place to the west of town. The cottage was the childhood home of Shakespeare's wife, Anne. Three miles (5km) to the northwest is **Mary Arden's Farm** (Station Road, Wilmcote; tel: 01789-204 016; www.shakespeare. org.uk; mid-Mar–Oct daily 10am–5pm; charge). Home to Shakespeare's grandparents and the childhood home of his mother, Mary Arden, there is

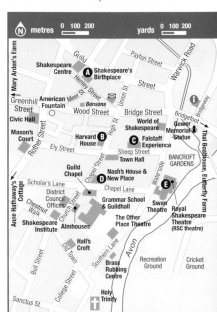

Above: an aspect of Hidcote Garden, created as a series of 'rooms'.

plenty to interest all the family, from a recreation of a Tudor farm to 16th-century entertainment, falconry, animal husbandry and nature trails.

To venture beyond the suburbs of Stratford take the B4632 south towards Mickleton.

NORTH COTSWOLDS

The pleasant village of **Mickleton** lies some 7 miles (11km) south of Stratford on the far northern end of the steep escarpment that marks the western edge of the Cotswold Hills. Its particular claim to fame was cauliflower-growing but it is now known as the home of the celebrated Pudding Club. Located in the attractive Three Ways House hotel *(see pp.85 and 126)*, you need to be a member to enjoy the club but if you have dinner at the hotel you will be able to try one of the delectable desserts.

Beautiful Gardens
To the east of Mickleton follow the signs up the steep hill through lovely countryside for Hidcote Manor Garden and Kiftsgate Court.

For garden lovers, the real highlight of the day is a visit to the celebrated **Hidcote Manor Garden ②** (tel: 01386-438 333; www.nationaltrust.org.uk;

May–Aug daily 9am–6pm, mid-Mar–Apr, Sept–Oct Sat–Wed 10am–5pm; charge), at Hidcote Bartrim.

These days there is something of a reaction against the kind of highly architectural garden that Hidcote pioneered, and young garden designers prefer a more naturalistic style, with a greater emphasis on plants grown in drifts, rather than using them to decorate outdoor rooms bounded by clipped yews and pleached limes. Few but the most hardened iconoclasts are immune to the charm of Hidcote in the flesh, however, and the garden will give encouragement and inspiration to anyone struggling to create their own patch of colour. This garden did not exist until 1907, created from an unpromising farmyard set high on a cold, exposed and windswept hill. The garden was still incomplete in 1948 when its creator, Lawrence Johnston, handed it over to the National Trust.

Another great garden to visit is just back down the road. At the same time that Johnston was devoting his life to Hidcote, Heather Muir was busy cre-

Above: a field on the outskirts of the old wool merchants' town of Chipping Campden.

ating the garden at **Kiftsgate Court** ❸ (tel: 01386-438 777; www.kifts gate.co.uk; May–July Sat–Wed noon– 6pm, Aug 2–6pm; Apr, Sept Sun– Mon, Wed 2–6pm; charge). Kiftsgate is synonymous with the Himalayan climbing rose known to the world as *Rosa filipes* 'Kiftsgate', a vigorous plant that is allowed to grow at will and flowers profusely in June. This is just one of a huge range of roses and oth- er plants that grow in the informal ter- raced gardens that run down the hill below the house. The latest addition is a stunning water garden created on the site of an old tennis court.

Above: Kiftsgate Court gardens, known for their climbing roses, in Mickleton.

Instead of going back down to Mickleton continue southeast to **Ebrington** *(see box, below)*, another achingly pretty Cotswold village. From Ebrington, travel south on a mi- nor road then west on the B4035 to Chipping Campden.

CHIPPING CAMPDEN

For many visitors, **Chipping Camp- den** ❹ is the quintessential Cotswold town, although it is, in many respects, utterly untypical, not least in having been beautifully preserved by the Campden Trust. Formed in 1929 by a group of local architects and crafts- men, the Trust has restored many

properties, and it sets high standards for the appearance of the town. Tele- graph and power cables are buried un- derground or brought into the backs of houses so that wires do not mar the appearance of the broad High Street, and intrusive modern shop fronts are not allowed. Chipping Campden is at the start of the national Cotswold Way Trail *(see box p.53)*.

Historic Buildings

Another unusual feature at Camp- den is the sheer variety of buildings in a plethora of different styles that have survived from all ages. One that

ⒻEbrington

It's worth stopping off or staying in Ebrington for its lovely architecture, interesting church and very good pub. The Norman church of St Fad- burgha has a stone font with seven decorated sides, and the striking painted effigy forms part of the tomb of Henry VI's Lord Chancellor, Sir John Fortescue, who was buried here in 1485. The Ebrington Arms is a historic 17th-century pub, perfect for a meal or a pint.

Above: a frosty dawn breaks in the village of Ebrington.

visitors see first is the dramatic gate-house to Campden Manor, built by Sir Baptist Hicks in 1613 in flamboyant Jacobean style, and then deliberately burned down by the Royalists during the Civil War to prevent it falling into the hands of the hated Parliamentarians. Hicks, himself a fierce Royalist, also built the fine block of almshouses opposite the manor gateway. Dating from 1612, the plan of the block makes the letter "I", in honour of King James (or Iames, as the name was sometimes spelt).

There is an imposing monument to Hicks (died 1629) in Campden's **Church of St James**, possibly carved by the great English Renaissance sculptor Nicholas Stone. The nave of the church (built by the same masons as Northleach Church, see p.96) is a triumph of the Perpendicular style, with its slender octagonal columns supporting a lofty roof, lit by large clerestory windows. The church has a number of brasses dating from the time when Campden was one of the Cotswolds' main wool markets. In front of the altar is one dedicated to a merchant who thrived on this trade: William Grevel (died 1401) is described in his epitaph as 'the flower of the wool merchants of England'.

The house that Grevel built in 1380 still survives in the High Street, on the right as you approach from Church Street; it is unmistakable because of its two-storeyed bay window. On the opposite side of the road is the stylish Bedfont House, a delightful classical building of the 1740s. Another building of note along the main street is the **Market Hall** dating from 1627, another gift to the town paid for by Sir Baptist Hicks. It looks like an Italian Renaissance loggia but with Cotswold-style gables.

Craft Shopping

A number of the shops in Campden are devoted to selling crafts and objects that exemplify good design (for example, Robert Welch's shop on the Lower High Street). This is, in part, a legacy of the Guild of Handicrafts that was established in East London in 1888 by C.R. Ashbee. Inspired by ideals of reviving craft traditions that gave men and women pride in their work, rather than making them merely

Below: the Church of St James, Chipping Campden.

Above: butter, cheese and poultry were sold in the old Market Hall.

Heritage Lottery funding to set up a **Museum of Craft and Design** (tel: 01386-841 951; www.courtbarn.org. uk; Tue–Sun Apr–Sept 10am–5pm, Oct–Mar 10am–4pm; charge), in the restored Court Barn near the church in Chipping Campden. This traces the history of crafts and design in the region from the Arts and Crafts movement to the present day.

View Over Campden and Beyond

Continue through the town and follow signs for **Dover's Hill**. It's just a short walk from the car park to one of the best views in the Cotswolds, or ask at the visitor information centre for a route to walk all the way up from the town. This spectacular natural amphitheatre provides views in every direction, down onto Campden to the southeast, to the Vale of Evesham to the northwest and over the Burnt Norton estate (which inspired T.S. Eliot's poem in the *Four Quartets*) to the north. This is also the setting for the Cotswold Olimpick Games, so called by Robert Dover after whom the hill is named. The eccentric Dover started the games in 1612 and they feature such rural sports as shin-kicking, climbing the greasy

adjuncts to machinery, Ashbee moved here from the Mile End Road with a group of East End families in 1902 and set up a workshop in the old Silk Mill in Sheep Street.

You can visit Guild Craft workshops including Hart Gold and Silversmiths (Mon–Fri 9am 5pm, Sat 9am–noon) founded by one of Ashbee's followers, George Hart, on the first floor. The Guild of Handicrafts secured

F National Gardens Scheme

There are many gardens open for charity in the Cotswolds under the National Gardens Scheme. It may only be once or twice each summer but well worth a look if you are in the vicinity, and some provide teas, too. Of particular interest are several wonderful gardens in the Blockley village group, some of which are open on the same day, usually in May or June. For details of all the gardens, visit www.ngs.org.uk.

Above: take tea surrounded by blossoms on an open garden day.

Above: the Norman parish church St Peter and St Paul stands in the pleasant village of Blockley.

pole and duelling with backswords (a polite name for wooden cudgels), all designed to be a training in 'the manly sports for the harmless mirthe and jollitie of the neighbourhood'. The games continued uninterrupted (except for a brief period during the Civil War) until 1852 when the rowdy behaviour of 'armed bands of beer-swilling Birmingham yahoos' got them banned. Revived in 1951, they now take place on the last weekend in May or the first in June, and are followed by a torchlit procession into Campden where the townspeople dance until late in the floodlit High Street (www.olimpickgames.co.uk).

VILLAGES AND GARDENS

From the centre of town, by the Red Lion pub, take the road signed to Broad Campden. Shortly after, turn left and continue on to the beautiful village of Broad Campden.

Broad Campden and Blockley

Entering the village of **Broad Campden ❺**, pass the Baker's Arms on the left with the house of C.R. Ashbee (*see p.80–1*) on the right; a delightful home converted from a ruined Norman chapel. The house is all but invis-

ible behind its high yew hedge topped by topiary birds, but the village is delightfully grouped around a green with a tiny house-sized church. Go up the hill out of the main village turning right for Blockley by Sedgecombe House.

Continuing south you will skirt Northwick Park to the east, with its splendid house dating from 1686 (now converted to apartments) before entering the attractive village of **Blockley ❻**. This village is built on a series of terraces above the deep valley of the Knee Brook. From the village you can look across to the open pasture on the opposite hill, grazed by sheep today as it was in medieval times when the bishops of Worcester cleared the village of Upton, moving its inhabitants in order to create more grazing for their vast flocks. Bumps in the pasture show quite clearly where the old houses used to stand.

Blockley was where the sheep were brought to be sheared before their wool was washed, spun and woven in the mills at the bottom of the valley. When overseas competition destroyed the local wool-processing

Below: sculpture in a shell-encrusted grotto at Mill Dene Garden.

Above: Bourton-on-the-Hill, straddling the main A44.

industry, local entrepreneurs converted their mills to the production of silk. As a result, several that still survive (now turned into private houses) have names like the Old Silk Mill or the Ribbon Mill. Wandering the maze of paths through the village, past brightly coloured front gardens, you will spot the former weavers' cottages by their attic windows; the grander houses belonged to the mill owners.

In the centre of Blockley is **Mill Dene Garden** (tel: 01386-700 457; www.milldenegarden.co.uk; Apr–June, Sept Wed–Fri 10am–5pm, Sat 9am–2-pm and bank holidays 11am–5.30pm; charge) with its beautiful stream garden planted around the water course that feeds the mill pool. From the top of the garden there are extensive views *(see box, right)*.

Bourton-on-the-Hill
Continue south on the B4479, turning east onto the A44 to **Bourton-on-the-Hill** (2 miles/3km), a fine village whose charms are difficult to appreciate fully because of heavy traffic. Here you can visit **Bourton House Garden** (tel: 01386-700 754; www.bourtonhouse.com; Apr–Oct Wed–Fri 10am–5pm; charge). This is a more conventional 3-acre (1-hectare) English

garden set around a handsome manor house with topiary, knot gardens and flamboyant borders stuffed full of unusual plants. As well as being open to the public, the garden serves as a venue for film shoots (most recently for Japanese TV in 2012) and charity events.

MORE NOTABLE COTSWOLD GARDENS
To the east just outside Bourton on the A44 there are two more fine gardens to visit and the order in which you visit them will depend on the day of the week and the time of day – be aware that Sezincote has more restricted hours than Batsford.

Ⓥ Garden With a View
The panoramas from the romantic Mill Dene Garden stretch across the beautiful rolling Cotswold landscape. The views from the fruit garden are especially fine and the herb garden has the village church as a backdrop. The garden, set around the mill, has been terraced up a steep sided valley, further enhancing the outlook from the top. There are plenty of seats on which to relax and take in the vista.

Above: the church can be seen from the Mill Dene herb garden.

Above: woods at Batsford Arboretum.

Sezincote

It is worth planning your trip to fit in the most spectacular garden, **Sezincote 7** (tel: 01386-700 444; www.sezincote.co.uk; garden: Jan–Nov Thur–Fri and bank holiday Mon 2–6pm or dusk, house: May–Sept Thur–Fri 2.30–5.30pm; charge), to the south of the A44. Sezincote is an exotic delight that ought not to fit into the Cotswold countryside but does so supremely well. Inspired by northern Indian temples and fortresses, it combines homely Cotswold features with chattris and chajas, peacock-tail windows and colonnades, statues of Brahmin bulls and a reproduction of Hyder Ali Khan's mausoleum. Put together, the result is a building so astonishing that the Prince Regent, visiting in 1807, told his architect to scrap all existing plans for the Brighton Pavilion, and 'build me something like

Sezincote'. Those who tour the house will discover that the oriental elements are all on the outside – inside it is a more conventional Regency house – but the building served its purpose in reminding the client, Sir Charles Cockerell, of his beloved India, where he had served for many years with the East India Company.

The gardens (among the finest in Gloucestershire) are built around a natural stream that bubbles out of the ground on the hill above, before being channelled by a series of pools and cascades through temples and between banks brimming with moisture-loving plants. Clumps of bamboo, delicate Japanese maples, weeping birches and beeches all thrive in these conditions, adding interest and continuing the oriental theme.

Batsford Arboretum

Batsford is another garden inspired by memories of the Orient. **Batsford Arboretum 8** (tel: 01386-701 441; www.batsarb.co.uk; daily 10am–5pm, until dusk in winter; charge), almost opposite the Sezincote entrance, was planted from 1886 by Lord Redesdale, who had been on diplomatic service in Tokyo. When he returned he planted his garden with the flowering cherries, magnolias and maples that are such a feature of Japanese landscapes. Spring and autumn are the best times to visit for colour, but the magnificent vistas and the garden centre make this a place worth visiting all year.

Also here is the **Cotswold Falconry Centre** (tel: 01386-701 043; www.cotswold-falconry.co.uk; mid-Feb–mid-Nov daily 10.30am–5pm; charge), where you can watch birds of prey in the aviaries through closed-circuit television, and view demonstrations as eagles, hawks, owls and

Left: Moreton-in-Marsh market.

falcons show off their hunting skills. There are flying displays at 11.30am, 1.30pm, 3pm and 4.30pm. Back on the A44 continue east to the town of Moreton-in-Marsh.

MORETON-IN-MARSH

Just 2 miles (3km) from Bourton, **Moreton-in-Marsh ❾** is a good place for refreshment as it is full of handsome former coaching inns, such as the Manor House Hotel of 1658, the White Hart of 1782 and the 18th-century Redesdale Arms *(see p.126)*. These grand old watering holes all cater for visitors who come to shop, especially on Tuesday, when a huge market fills the long, broad main street. Buildings of note in the town include the Curfew Tower, opposite the Market Hall. It was built in the 16th century and used to ring the curfew every night until 1860, warning householders to cover their fires, a necessary precaution in the days when timber buildings regularly burned to the ground in the night because of stray sparks.

The **Wellington Aviation Museum** (Broadway Road; tel: 01608-650 323; www.wellingtonaviation.org; Tue–Sun 10am–12.30pm, 2–5pm; charge), is small but crammed full of aviation memorabilia and information. Moreton-in-Marsh was a training centre for RAF Bomber Command.

Ⓔ Eating Out

Stratford-upon-Avon
Bensons
4 Bard's Walk; tel: 01789-261 116; www.bensonsrestaurant.co.uk; Mon–Sat 9am–5pm, Sun 10am–5pm.
Come for breakfast, coffee and cakes, full lunch or afternoon tea. Huge range of traditional and herbal teas. Treat yourself to a special champagne breakfast or tea. £–££

Thai Boathouse
Swan's Nest Lane; tel: 01789-297 733; www.thai.group.co.uk; daily noon–2.30pm, 5.30–10.30pm (closed Sat lunch).
Nicely located above a boathouse by the river. Lovely Thai furniture and ornaments complement the first-class authentic Thai food – the chicken curry is exceptional. ££

Mickleton
Three Ways House Restaurant
Mickleton; tel: 01386-438 429; www.threewayshousehotel.com; restaurant Sun 12.30–2.30pm, 7–9pm, Mon–Sat 7–9pm; brasserie daily noon–2.30pm, 7–9pm
Award-winning hotel restaurant and more informal Bar Brasserie. Local produce is used to create dishes such as braised spiced pork belly with creamed Savoy cabbage and bacon. ££–£££

Chipping Campden
Badgers Hall
High Street; tel: 01386-840 839; www.badgershall.com; Mon–Sat 10am–4.30pm (last orders), Sun 11am–4.30pm.
A quintessential English tearoom, Badgers Hall occupies a 15th-century Cotswold-stone house. Delicious cakes complement the unforgettable cream teas. £

Moreton-in-Marsh
Marshmallow Restaurant and Tea Rooms
High Street; tel: 01608 651 536; www.marshmallow-tea-restaurant.co.uk; Mon 8.30am–early evening, Tue 10am–4pm, Wed–Sat 8.30am–8pm (Fri, Sat until 8.30pm), Sun 10.30am–early evening
Lovely restaurant and tearoom with an outside terrace. The special afternoon tea is particularly good, with an interesting choice of teas. ££

Morris Dancing

A predominantly male dance troupe clad in white, skipping, banging wooden sticks and waving flags is an interesting sight deserving some explanation

Morris dancing is found all over England, but it is particularly associated with the Cotswolds area (mostly in Gloucestershire and Oxfordshire), where the most evolved form was, and still is, to be found.

THE ORIGINS

One of the oldest English traditions, Morris dancing dates back at least to the 15th century, but could perhaps be much older. It is believed this form of English folk dance originated as part of ritual dancing found throughout most of Europe and particularly Moorish dancing from Spain. Hence, from Moorish evolved the name 'Morris'.

THE COTSWOLD VERSION

The dance has evolved in six prominent styles determined by the part of the country it originates from. The Cotswolds' version is performed by six men and a musician, accompanied in most cases by a 'fool' and sometimes a 'beast'. The men are dressed in costume consisting of a white shirt and trousers, and a hat adorned with flowers and ribbons. Garters are worn around the legs with

dances and tunes but by the end of the Industrial Revolution Morris dancing had almost died out.

A GREAT REVIVAL

In late Victorian England a movement began in an attempt to emphasise traditional values and the benefits of rural living – a reaction against industrialism and the expanding urban society. This in turn created groups such as conservation societies – which were to grow into the National Trust – and fortunately among these groups was one dedicated to the preservation of Morris dancing.

CECIL SHARP

Music teacher Cecil Sharp recognised the importance of traditional English music and song and in 1904 he published *Folk Songs from Somerset*. Because of this, he was invited to join the committee of the Folk Song Society. Cecil Sharp's other main interest was in dance and in this he was a pioneer. He researched country dance, sword and Morris dancing, and in 1911 he founded the English Folk Dance Society. By bringing together traditional song and dance, he awakened a modern interest in Morris.

bells attached and handkerchiefs or sticks are waved. A fiddle or concertina provides the music.

The dance often illustrates a legend or a rural activity such as sowing and harvesting and the bells and handkerchiefs are to ward off evil spirits and to ensure fertility of the crops for the coming year. In the past, most Cotswold villages associated with the tradition had their own individual

THE PRESENT DAY

Nowadays, each spring and summer you are still able to see Morris dancers entertaining with much enthusiasm and vibrancy in Cotswold town squares and on village greens, ensuring this old English tradition lives forever. For those interested in catching a performance, the Gloucestershire Morris Men (www.glosmorrismen.org) are one group to watch out for. Formed from what remained of a revival Morris side that started in Cheltenham in the 1930s, they can be seen dancing at various events across the region and also at many local pubs.

Above: Morris men perform in Bledington. **Top Left**: performance outside a village pub. **Centre Left**: traditional concertina. **Left**: bells are strapped below the knees.

Tour 7

Around Stow-on-the-Wold

Starting in the Oxfordshire Cotswolds, this 60-mile (96km) full-day tour takes you to some of the most popular tourist destinations in the area, as well as a few secret corners

Centred on Stow-on-the-Wold, the tour begins in Oxfordshire at Chipping Norton on the edge of the Cotswolds area. It takes in two ancient sights, at Rollright and Chedworth, some quintessential villages and towns, the tourist honeypot of Bourton-on-the-Water, with plenty for the children, and the rare breeds centre, Cotswold Farm Park.

CHIPPING NORTON AND AROUND

The town of **Chipping Norton ❶**, perched on the highest point in Oxfordshire, was once a centre for the

Above: the King's Men circle, part of the Rollright Stones near Chipping Norton.

Highlights

- Chipping Norton
- Rollright Stones
- Stow-on-the-Wold
- The Slaughters
- Cotswold Farm Park
- Bourton-on-the-Water
- Northleach
- Chedworth Roman Villa

Cotswold wool trade. The town has a strong local community spirit and several independent businesses, including antique shops. To find out more of its local history visit Chipping Norton Museum (High Street, tel: 01608-641 712; Easter–Oct Mon–Sat 2–4pm; charge).

East of the heart of the Cotswolds, the Oxfordshire Cotswolds are worth a visit. The main centres are Chipping Norton *(see p.88)* and Burford *(see p.104)*, and further east the towns of Witney, Charlbury and Woodstock. In between are pretty villages and enchanting countryside, perfect for walkers and cyclists. Rivers, too, play an important part – the Thames and the pretty, wild Windrush. See www. oxfordshirecotswolds.org.

Above: town centre view of the Oxfordshire town of Chipping Norton.

Rollright Stones

From Chipping Norton take the B4026 north, and after about half a mile (1km) turn left in Over Norton and follow signs to the **Rollright Stones** ❷ (www.rollrightstones. co.uk; daily sunrise–sunset; small charge in honesty box), which are administered by the Rollright Trust. Located on the right-hand side of the road, they are accessed from a lay-by through a gate in the hedge. The King's Men circle, made up of 77 stones, dates to about 2500– 2000 BC, and according to folklore

represents the petrified remains of a king and his knights. Across the field four stones represent the Whispering Knights and over the road a single stone is named the King's Stone.

Chastleton House

Turn round with care and continue southwest towards Little Compton and at the junction with the A44 turn right for Evesham. Almost immediately turn left onto the A436 for Stow. After 1 mile (2km) turn right to visit **Chastleton House** (tel: 01494-755 560; www.nationaltrust.org.uk; Wed–

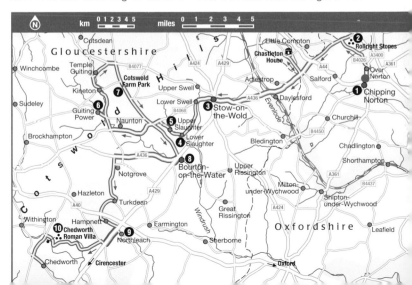

Sat late Apr–Sept 1–5pm, mid-Mar–end Mar, Oct 1–4pm; charge, timed tickets). This is one of England's finest and most perfect Jacobean houses, which remained virtually untouched for nearly 400 years. It was acquired by the National Trust in the mid-1990s and is wonderfully atmospheric, even down to the ceiling in the old kitchen, which has never been cleaned. The gardens are a delight, and include a lawn where the rules of modern croquet were laid down in 1865.

STOW-ON-THE-WOLD

Return to the A436 for Stow. Just west off this road is the village of Adlestrop made famous in a poem by Edward Thomas *(see box p.91)*. **Stow-on-the-Wold ❸**, according to an ancient rhyme, is 'where the wind blows cold'. The truth of this becomes chill-

Above: the stocks on the green in Stow-on-the-Wold.

Ⓢ Shopping in Stow

Stow-on-the-Wold is a magnet for shoppers in the Cotswolds with antique shops, galleries, fine food delis, independent boutiques and furniture stores. Classic lines and country styles abound, with stylish gifts from the Cotswolds also on sale; there is little that is tacky. The town is the home of the flagship Scotts of Stow, with everything for the kitchen and home.

Above: antiques and fine arts for sale in Stow.

ingly apparent if you visit Stow, the Cotswolds' highest town (situated at around 754ft/230 metres) on a grey day in February, but in summer the town has a festive atmosphere, packed with coach-trippers and antique hunters coming to browse in the town's good art and antique galleries *(see box, left)*.

Stow's huge market square testifies to the size of the flocks that used to be driven here for sale between 1107 (when Henry I granted the town its charter) and the 1980s, when the Stow Horse Fairs were moved away from the town because of the crime and chaos they created. Wooden stocks survive on the green in Stow's marketplace as a warning to miscreants.

Stow's **church** contains memorials to several of those who died in the last (and perhaps the fiercest) battle of the Civil War, which took place on 21 March 1646. The church was used as a prison and held some 1,000-plus Royalists at one time, suffering much damage as a result. The curious north porch, which has two yew trees flanking the doorway growing out of the masonry, was added as part of the

Ⓕ Remembering Adlestrop

The village of Adlestrop was immortalised in an eponymous poem by the celebrated World War I poet Edward Thomas. He was travelling on a train that made an unscheduled stop at the station just before the war that was to claim his life began. The station is now long gone but the poem is inscribed on a plaque in Adlestrop's bus shelter beneath the sign salvaged from the old station.

Above: the old station sign is now situated in the village bus shelter.

1680 restoration. Inside there is a fine slate floor memorial near the altar to the Royalist Hastings Keyt, dressed in uniform sash and helmet. Easily missed at the back of the church is a naturalistically carved hare, part of a Saxon carving from the first church on the site, founded in AD 986.

PERFECT COTSWOLD VILLAGES

Surrounding Stow are some of the Cotswolds' prettiest villages. One

Above: yew-lined path leading to the delightful Norman church at Upper Slaughter

mile (1.5km) west on the B4068 and reached by leaving Stow by going over the crossroads with the A429 (no sign, but opposite the Unicorn Hotel) is the village of **Lower Swell**. This name perhaps refers to the ancient well in the village. There are also some remarkable Norman carvings in its generally over-restored church. There's a village war memorial designed by Edwin Lutyens, who was also the architect of nearby Abbotswood house, which can be seen when the excellent gardens are open under the National Gardens Scheme (see box p.81).

The Slaughters

Go through the village following signs for The Slaughters, past the Golden Ball pub and then bear left for **Lower Slaughter Ⓞ**. The village is almost too perfect, and the slough (or marsh) from which the village derives its name has been tidied up, so that the River Eye now flows between grassy banks and colourful cottage gardens beneath a series of stone bridges. At the western end of the village you can visit the Old Mill (tel: 01451-820 052; www.oldmill-lowerslaughter.com; daily 10am–6pm; charge), last used commercially in 1958. There is a mill museum, craft shop and tearooms

Above: a line of handsome terraces on the green at Guiting Power.

(see p.97), as well as a parlour famous for its home-made ice cream.

A delightful lane follows the Eye upstream to **Upper Slaughter** ❺, with a good view on the right of the Elizabethan manor (now Lords of the Manor Hotel, see p.125) as you enter the village. The church has fine Norman details, but its most curious feature is the large, mock-medieval tomb of the Reverend F.E. Witts (died

Above: rolling pastures near Temple Guiting.

1854), whose *Diary of a Cotswold Parson* was discovered some years ago.

For a short but interesting walk through the village, take the left-hand path from the church and turn left to reach the point where the Eye forms a ford. Turn right by the ford and follow the trout-filled stream, past banks of bullrushes and waterside plants where dragonflies dart. Turn right uphill once the path meets the road to return to the village green in front of the church. Turning right from the church, take the road signposted to Cheltenham, bringing you to the B4068. Turn left and continue on the road to **Naunton**, 4 miles (6.5km) west, which passes through a valley filled with the kinds of flowers that only grow on unimproved limestone pasture – cowslips in spring, yellow rattle and rare orchids in summer. The village church has an interesting monument to Ambrose Oldys, vicar of Adderbury in Oxfordshire, who was 'barbarously murthered by ye rebells' in 1645. The inscription tells of his unshakeable loyalty to the Crown and his adherence to the established Church. Volunteers have restored the lovely dovecote in the village.

The Guitings

Passing Naunton church take the steep uphill road, turning right at the top, and follow signs for **Guiting Power ⑥**, another handsome village, with a fine 15th-century cross carved with the Virgin and Child and the Crucifixion standing on the green. The handsome cruciform church has an hourglass carved in stone over the doorway to remind us of the brevity of life and there are a variety of humorous portrait heads carved on the roof supports inside.

Just over a mile (2km) to the north through Kineton, **Temple Guiting** (so called because it once belonged to the Knights Templar) is not as pretty, but its church does have a fine 18th-century nave and an intricately modelled plaster coat of arms of George II, flanked by a rampant lion and unicorn. The church can be found by turning right opposite the school, some 50 yds/metres down, set back from the road on the right. From the village continue on to the B4077 and at the crossroads turn right for Bourton-on-the-Water.

COTSWOLD FARM PARK

Just over a mile (2km) to the south is the **Cotswold Farm Park ⑦** (tel: 01451-850 307; www.cotswoldfarm park.co.uk; daily mid-Mar–mid-Oct 10.30am–5pm, Nov–mid-Dec, early Feb–mid-Mar 10.30am–4pm; charge). Founded by Joe Henson in 1970, this was the first farm in England to specialise in the rescue of rare breeds of farm animal, and is now run by Joe's son, Adam, who also presents a farm-based segment weekly on the BBC programme *Countryfile*. Some of the animals here were only recently rescued from extinction: the White Park Cattle, for example, an ancient Celtic (pre-Roman) strain once bred for hunting and for ornament, and the

Above: roadside vendor in Bourton-on-the-Water.

Norfolk Horn Sheep (down to the last four rams and five ewes before a breeding programme was initiated).

For young visitors, the real appeal of the Cotswold Farm Park is that the animals are nearly all friendly, contented and placid. The Touch Barn offers the chance for the family to make friends with small animals such as rabbits, ducklings and baby goats and it is possible to bottle-feed animals, too. Other attractions for youngsters are the Jumping Pillows, Lion Maze, Adventure Playground, Farm Safari and the Wildlife Walk.

BOURTON-ON-THE-WATER

Another cluster of children's attractions can be found in **Bourton-on-the-Water ⑧**, 6 miles (10km) south. This whole village (www.bourtoninfo. com) is given over to tourism, but even the tacky gift shops do not detract from the charm of what has been dubbed 'the Venice of the Cotswolds' because of the elegant 18th-century bridges that cross the River Windrush as it flows through the centre of the village. One of Bourton's best attractions is the enchanting **Model Village** at the Old New Inn in the High Street (tel: 01451-820 467; www.theoldnew

Above: Bourton-on-the-Water is known as the 'Venice of the Cotswolds'.

inn.co.uk/village; daily late Mar–late Oct 10am–6pm, late Oct–late Mar 10am–4pm; charge) depicting Bourton (as it was in 1937) at one-ninth scale. Keep an eye out for novel features such as the bonsai trees, and the choir and organ music just discernible if you put your ear to the door of the parish church.

Close by in Rissington Road is **Birdland** (tel: 01451-820 480; www. birdland.co.uk; Apr–Oct daily 10am–6pm, Nov–Mar until 4pm; charge). The best time to visit is at around 2.30pm when the 500 or so birds are fed, from the fruit-eating parrots to the fish-eating penguins. Most of the birds here were bred at the park and they are so tame that they are allowed to wander freely. The indoor Discovery Zone is a bonus in wet weather.

Bourton's other attractions include the **Bourton Model Railway** (Box Bush, High Street; tel: 01451-820 686; www.bourtonmodelrailway.co.uk; June–Aug daily 11am–5pm, Sept–May Sat–Sun 11am–5pm, Jan limited hours; charge) which will entertain anyone with nostalgic yearnings for the train set of their youth; the **Cotswold Perfumery** (tel: 01451-

820 698; www.cotswold-perfumery. co.uk; Mon–Sat 9.30am–5pm, Sun 10.30am–5pm; charge for factory tours), just over the river, with exhibits and a programme on how perfumes are made; and the **Cotswold Motoring Museum and Toy Collection** (Sherbourne Street; tel: 01451-821 255; www.cotswold motoringmuseum.co.uk; Feb–Oct daily 10am–6pm; charge). The latter is the home of Brum, which younger children will recognise as the little yellow car that features in the television

Below: relaxing by the banks of the Windrush on a warm summer's day.

Above: the Norman church of St Bartholomew in Notgrove.

programme of the same name. The museum is also an Aladdin's cave of motoring memorabilia.

As an antidote to museums, your children might enjoy visiting the **Dragonfly Maze** (Rissington Road; tel: 01451-822 251; www.thedragonflymaze.com; daily Apr–Sept 10am–5pm, Oct–Mar times vary so call to check; charge) with its labyrinth of yew-lined pathways and intriguing clues. Or you can explore **Salmonsbury Meadows Nature Reserve** (tel: 01452-383 333; daily; free) located on the edge of Bourton off Station Road, a meadow-

land along the tiny River Eye. Look out for roe deer and foxes, water voles and rare orchids *(see box, below)*.

CHURCHES AND VILLAGES

From Bourton, you can either take the direct road to Northleach along the A429 Fosse Way, or you can meander through three of the least-spoiled villages to be found in the Cotswolds – Notgrove, Turkdean and Hampnett – leaving Bourton westwards on the A436 signposted to Cheltenham.

Notgrove and Turkdean

The idyllic setting of **Notgrove** church (4 miles/6km south off A436) alone makes it worth a visit, but other treasures include a tapestry made in 1954 showing the village, church and manor glimpsed through hazel trees (a reference to the village name), and a lovely stained-glass fragment from *c.*1300, depicting the Virgin and Child. From the church continue up to the main road turning left for **Turkdean**, where the church in the middle of the village is an architectural puzzle, a patchwork of Norman masonry, the remains of a 15th-century St Christopher wall painting and stained glass added in 1924. Continuing downhill, cross the ford and head southwest to Hampnett.

Ⓖ Greystones and Salmonsbury

This site, where farming has been part of the landscape for 6,000 years, is managed by Gloucestershire Wildlife Trust and covers 163 acres (66 hectares). Archaeological remains can be seen behind Greystones Farm. Salmonsbury Meadows is designated a Site of Scientific Importance for its natural habitat, one of the largest and richest in the Cotswolds with rare wild plants and a stretch of the River Eye.

Above: Gloucestershire Wildlife Trust supporters at Greystones Farm.

Hampnett

Across the A40 is Hampnett, which looks as if time stopped here some time in the pre-industrial age, with its farmhouses grouped around a rough green where the River Leach springs out of the ground and begins its journey to join the Thames at Lechlade. The church, with its Norman carvings of birds on the chancel-arch capitals, is made more delightful by the 19th-century wall paintings, executed by the rector, the Reverend Wiggin, in an attempt to re-create the original Norman appearance. Pass the church and continue to meet the A429.

Above: mellow facades at Hampnett.

Northleach

The road from Hampnett joins the A429 just above the Old Prison (on the right) at **Northleach ❾**, adjacent to which is a centre with an exhibition produced by the Cotswold Conservation Board, depicting the Cotswolds Area of Outstanding Natural Beauty. Built in 1791, the prison reflected the reforming ideas of local philanthropist, Sir George Onesiphorus Paul, and it set new standards

Below: welcome to a world of mechanical music.

for prison health and hygiene. The cell block and courthouse holds the Lloyd Baker Cotswold Rural Collection of Agricultural Carts (tel: 01451-862 000; Apr–Oct Wed–Sat 11am–4pm; free).

By contrast, turn left at the traffic lights for the town centre and **Keith Harding's World of Mechanical Music** (High Street; tel: 01451-860 181; www.mechanicalmusic.co.uk; daily 10am–5pm; charge), which is concerned with the intricate niceties of antique musical boxes and clocks, self-playing pianos and early gramophones. From the museum it is a short step up the churchyard path to one of the Cotswolds' finest churches, built with profits from the wool trade. Evidence of the industry is found throughout the church; the printed guide will tell you where to find fine 15th-century brasses decorated with sheep, woolsacks, woolmarks and shears. Some have dates in Arabic numerals, indicating trade contact with Spain and North Africa. Best of all is the Fortey brass, with its border decorated with slugs, snails, hedgehogs and strawberries. From Northleach take the A429 heading south towards Cirencester.

CHEDWORTH

Signs off the A429 will direct you to the remains of **Chedworth Roman Villa** ❿ (tel: 01242-890 256; www. nationaltrust.org.uk; daily Apr–Oct 10am–5pm, Nov, Feb–Mar 10am–4pm; charge), delightfully set in a wooded combe overlooking the Coln Valley. The mosaics here include a charming depiction of the seasons, with winter personified as a peasant in a billowing hooded cloak, bringing home a hare for the pot and a branch for fuel. In one corner of the site is a nymphaeum, a small sanctuary to the goddess of the spring that supplied the villa and its bathhouse with water. The Roman inhabitants introduced the edible snails that are found in and around the villa, especially on damp days, and which inhabit the railway cuttings above the villa, now a nature reserve.

Return to the road, turn left towards Withington and at the staggered crossroads turn sharp left and follow signs to the village of **Chedworth**. The church (on the left at the top of the hill as you enter the village) is another handsome Norman building, and its stone-carved 15th-century pulpit is one of the finest in the Cotswolds. Not far away is the atmospheric Seven Tuns pub, with an outdoor terrace and excellent food – the perfect place to contemplate the way in which the houses of Chedworth seem to cling to a series of terraces above the Coln Valley.

Ⓔ Eating Out

Chipping Norton
Wild Thyme Restaurant
10 New Street; tel: 01608-645 060; www.wildthymerestaurant.co.uk; Tue–Sat noon–2pm, 7–9pm.
This established local favourite serves modern British food with Mediterranean influences. Local seasonal produce is used, such as pigeon, venison and wild rabbit. £££

Stow-on-the-Wold
The Vine Leaf
10 Talbot Court; tel: 01451-832 010; www.thevineleaf.co.uk; Tue–Sat 11am–9pm, Sun 11am–5pm (summer only).
Locally sourced food served throughout the day. Look out for specials and set menus. Tables outside for summer eating. £ ££

Lower Slaughter
Old Mill
Mill Lane; tel: tel: 01451-820 052; www.oldmill-lowerslaughter.com; Apr–Oct daily 10am–6pm, check for winter times.
Pleasant riverside complex with a museum, tearoom and ice-cream parlour, gift and craft shop Treat yourself to organic ice-cream delights including summer berries, ground coffee or butter crunch flavours. £

Bourton-on-the-Water
The Croft
Victoria Street; tel: 01451-821 132; daily 9am–6pm, evening menu Thur–Mon 6–8pm, Sat until 9pm.
Located in Chester House B&B, The Croft has lovely river views; ideal for light bites or full meals. Booking advised for dinner. £–££

Northleach
The Wheatsheaf
West End; tel: 01451-860 244; www.cotswoldswheatsheaf.com; Mon–Sat noon–2.30pm, 6–9.30pm (until 10pm Fri–Sat), Sun noon–3pm.
Appealing to locals and visitors alike, the pub was refurbished in 2011. Mains range from beer battered whiting to mouth-watering steaks, served with a choice of sauces. Round off with a vanilla crème brûlée or Black Forest sundae. ££

Tour 8

The Coln and Windrush Valleys

This 60-mile (96km) full-day drive celebrates the beauty of the lesser-known Cotswolds, with delightful villages and their beautiful churches set amid rivers, hills and valleys

Many of the brooks, streams and rivers that rise in the high Cotswolds are tributaries of the Thames. Nearly all of them meet in a network of silvery threads in and around the town of Lechlade, where the slope of the Cotswold limestone meets the gravels of the Thames Valley. Springs and a plentiful supply of fresh water mean that these valleys have been settled since the earliest times.

VILLAGES AND THEIR CHURCHES

Most villages on this route have late Saxon churches, such as the fine example at **Ampney Crucis ❶**, 3 miles (5km) east of Cirencester,

just off the A417. Gone are the 14th-century wall paintings, but a copy of one still hangs in the tower, showing the particularly gruesome martyrdom of St Erasmus, his intestines wound

Left: Minster Lovell's church. **Above**: the tomb of George Lloyd in the late Saxon church at Ampney Crucis.

round a windlass. The main highlight is the flamboyant tomb of George Lloyd (died 1584) with its pedimented canopy, looking like a miniature temple.

Back on the A417, a short way down is a short stretch of dual carriageway. Here, to the right, is the church at **Ampney St Mary**, which stands alone in fields beside the Ampney Brook. The original village was abandoned in 1348, when it was struck by plague, and a new village was created a mile (1.5km) to the northeast. An intriguing Norman sculpture on the north wall depicts the triumph of good, in the form of a lion, over evil, a two-headed serpent. The 14th-century wall paintings within depict St Christopher, St George and the Dragon, and a Christ of the Trades, a symbolic mural representing the wounds inflicted on Christ by those who work on the Sabbath.

Also Saxon, though considerably enlarged in the 19th century, is the delightfully situated church at **Ampney St Peter**, a little further just north off the A417. Restorers spared the licentious carving (known as a sheela-na-gig) on the west wall of the nave,

though by that time the genitals had probably already been hacked off! Return to the A417 and continue east turning left by the Red Lion, signposted to Quenington.

Quenington

A long, relatively straight road northeast leads to **Quenington ❷**. Go through the main village, taking a right to where the church and the mill form a fine group with the 13th-century gateway to Quenington Court, once a Commandery of the Knights Hospitaller. Much of the interest at Quenington lies in the Romanesque carvings round the north and south doorways, so do not worry if the church is locked. The south door has a vigorous carving of the Harrowing of Hell; Christ appears thrusting a spear into the mouth of a figure representing Hell, while praying figures rise from the dead. The opposite door shows the Coronation of the Virgin, with Christ seated in Majesty surrounded by symbols of the Evangelists, and a beautiful domed building that represents the New Jerusalem, or the Temple of Heaven. Beakheads, a rare Romanesque feature, surround the

---

Ⓖ Thames Path

Opened in 1996, the path follows the Thames for 184 miles (296km) from its source at Kemble, Gloucestershire to the Thames Barrier near Woolwich, London. The entire length can be walked, but not cycled (check for cycling sections on www.nationaltrail. co.uk/thamespath). It is possible to access several parts of the route by public transport. Much of the route runs through delightful Cotswold countryside, with plenty of places to stay along the way.

Above: the church doorway at Coln St Alwyns draws the eye with its stylised designs.

arch; among the usual dragons and monsters are more familiar creatures, including a horse, a hare and a badger. Return to the village and take a right turn diagonally across the green.

Coln St Aldwyns

Upstream lies **Coln St Aldwyns**, an estate village that benefited greatly from the funds poured into it by the local squire, Sir Michael Hicks-Beach (1837–1916), a former chancellor of the exchequer. Hicks-Beach's house was substantially reduced in size after the war, and some of the timber

and stone was used to build the fine pedimented row of estate cottages opposite the church to your left. It is the doorway of the church that again commands attention, with its bold and deeply undercut chevron mouldings and two fine dragonhead stops.

Hatherop

To reach neighbouring **Hatherop** go over the crossroads in Coln. Here Lord de Mauley's French Gothic house is now a school. Reached by a long path, the church is in the school grounds (built in the 1850s) and is remarkable for the mortuary chapel of Barbara, Lady de Mauley (died 1844) at the south end of the church, depicted in a lovingly sculpted monument by Raffaelle Monti, with praying angels at her head and feet. The chapel itself is carved with a stone frieze in which wild flowers, butterflies and the letter 'B' for Barbara are intertwined.

Fairford

Follow Fairford signs from Hatherop and, on reaching the junction with the A417, turn right for **Fairford ❸**, which glories in perhaps the finest of all the Cotswold wool churches. It is

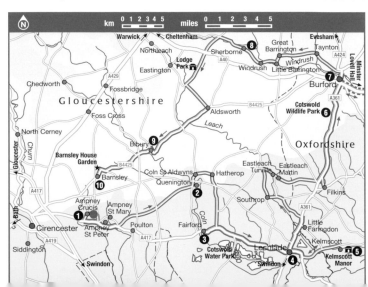

Above: Fairford church is renowned for its 15th-century stained glass depicting the whole biblical story.

reached by turning right into the main square. It was built at the expense of the local wool merchants, John and Edmund Tame.

Of primary interest is the almost complete sequence of 15th-century stained glass made in the workshops of Barnard Flower, master glass painter to Henry VII and the man who created the glass for Westminster Abbey's Lady Chapel. The whole biblical story, from the Creation to the Crucifixion, is depicted here, although it is the Last Judgement window, with its fiery red devils, that holds the most interest (bring binoculars to enjoy the grim details of diabolical punishment and torture). Of great importance, too, is the woodwork of the chancel screen (dating from 1501 27, and featuring carved pomegranates, the emblem of Catherine of Aragon, wife first of Prince Arthur and then of Arthur's younger brother, Henry VIII) and the misericords depicting scenes from popular fables, such as the story of Reynard the Fox. Among several fine tombs in the churchyard, look for the grave of Tiddles, the church cat. Fair-

ford hosts the world's largest military air show, the Royal International Air Tattoo, held annually in July. Return to the A417 and continue east.

LECHLADE

Lechlade ❹, 5 miles (8km) east of Fairford, has a church that inspired Shelley to write the sonnet *A Summer Evening Churchyard* in 1815. Lechlade marked the end of a holiday in which the poet had rowed up the Thames from Windsor. The footpath he took from the river to the town is now an attractive tree-lined path called, inevitably, Shelley's Walk (also known as Bridge Walk). It is worth following in his footsteps across the fields to St John's Bridge for a fine view of Lechlade's graceful church spire rising above the water meadows. St John's Bridge marks the highest navigable point along the river, and the bridge itself, although 19th-century, stands on the site of one of the earliest stone bridges to be built across the Thames. Beside the nearby lock is a stone statue of Old Father Thames, carved by Rafaelle Monti, sculptor of the Hatherop

Below: narrow boat moored at the meadow embankment at Lechlade.

Above: Kelmscott Manor was the summer residence of William Morris, artist, writer and co-founder of the Arts and Crafts Movement.

effigy. The slightly hidden path can be found opposite the pleasant Trout Inn, just beyond the sign to Kelmscott and marked Public Footpath. At the pub you can hire boats of various kinds from Cotswold Boat Hire (tel: 01793-727 083; www.cotswoldboat.co.uk).

Above: ornate enamel sign on an old post box in Lechlade.

Lechlade has plenty of walking opportunities and is on the excellent Thames Path route *(see box, p.99)*.

KELMSCOTT

The minor road alongside the pub heads through flat fields to the pretty village of **Kelmscott** where the **manor** ❺ is famous as the summer residence of William Morris *(see box p.103)* between 1871 and 1896 (tel: 01367-252 486; www.kelmscott manor.co.uk; Apr–Oct Wed and Sat 11am–5pm; charge). The house contains Morris' furniture, textiles and carpets; the gardens are delightful; and the barn beside the manor offers a comprehensive account of Morris and his time at Kelmscott.

Several buildings in the village exemplify the arts and crafts tradition that Morris founded, including the Morris Cottages (built by Jane Morris as a memorial to her husband in 1902), with a relief of Morris carved in stone on the facade: and the village hall, designed by Ernest Gimson. Jane and William Morris share a grave beneath a simple stone tomb in the

Above: reflections in the river at Eastleach.

rustic village churchyard, designed to resemble a Viking tomb-house.

REMOTE VILLAGES

Returning to Lechlade and heading north out of town on the A361 for about 1 mile (1.5km), take a signed turning (Southrop and Hatherop) to the west just beyond Little Faringdon to reach the valley of the River Leach and Southrop.

Southrop

The church at **Southrop** is on the left as you enter the village, and noted for its unusual Norman font, carved with armoured figures representing the Virtues trampling on beasts that represent the Vices. The names of the Virtues are carved in the arches above, while the names of the Vices are in mirror writing below, as if to emphasise the polarity of each Vice to its corresponding Virtue.

Eastleach

Many fine houses, surrounded by beautifully laid stone walls and threaded by the gentle river, make Southrop

one of the most attractive villages in the area, though there is strong competition from **Eastleach Turville** and **Eastleach Martin**, just to the north – reached by turning right just beyond the Swan pub. Here the two parish churches stand almost next to each other on opposite banks of the river, linked by an ancient stone clapper bridge downhill through the village. The peace here is delightful, far from the busy towns and tourist hotspots. The village also has the excellent Victoria Inn (see p.109), situated high up on the left as you come through the village – the perfect place to stop for a drink or lunch, with lovely views and possibly some lively local banter.

F Liaison at Kelmscott

In 1869, William Morris and Dante Gabriel Rossetti rented Kelmscott Manor as a summer retreat, but it soon became a hideaway for Rossetti and Morris' wife, Jane, to conduct a long-lasting and complicated liaison. The two spent summers there, with the Morris children, while Morris travelled abroad. Despite the unhappy marriage, Morris retained his love of the house and surrounding countryside until his death in 1896.

Above: high summer at the retreat of Kelmscott Manor.

Above: a rhino grazes at Cotswold Wildlife Park.

WEAVERS AND WILDLIFE

Follow the road east keeping to the right, signposted Burford, and at the junction with A361 turn right to reach the pretty village of **Filkins**.

Cotswold Woollen Weavers

Turn left in the village for the **Cotswold Woollen Weavers** (tel: 01367-860 600; www.cotswoldwoollenweavers. co.uk; Mon–Sat 10am–6pm, Sun 2–6pm; free). Here, in a splendid, traditional working mill, you can watch craftsmen spinning and weaving fleece into woollen fabric using age-old skills, and visit the well-stocked shop. Turn left out of the mill for the A361.

Filkins is also home to the Swinford Museum (Fox House; tel: 01367-860 504; May–Sept 1st and 3rd Sun in the month 2–5pm; free), one of Oxfordshire's oldest small museums, set up by George Swinford in the 1930s. Each year different exhibitions are displayed, often relating to the village of Filkins. On permanent display are local agricultural, craft and domestic items from the village's rich past.

Cotswold Wildlife Park

Three miles (5km) north is the **Cotswold Wildlife Park** ❻ (tel: 01993-823 006; www.cotswoldwildlifepark.

co.uk; daily Apr–Oct 10am–6pm, Nov–Mar 10am–5, or dusk (last admission 90 minutes before closing); charge). This is the perfect place to spend a day with children *(see box p.105)*, enjoying its narrow-gauge railway, children's farmyard, reptile houses and aquarium, not to mention the incongruous sight of zebras, rhinos and tigers roaming in Cotswold paddocks in front of a Gothic-style manor house. Conservation and breeding programmes are to the forefront and animals can also be 'adopted' thereby helping with the high costs for maintaining the park and its animals. The park is set in 160 acres (65 hectares) and also has superb gardens, including a Victorian walled kitchen garden.

BURFORD

Four miles (6.5km) to the north of the park is **Burford** ❼. It may be described as over-commercialised, but its charms should not be ignored. Often referred to as the 'Gateway to the Cotswolds' it is part of the region designated the Oxfordshire Cotswolds *(see box, p.89)*. It has

Above: the nave of St John the Baptist church, Burford.

Above: Burford, the 'Gateway to the Cotswolds', its high street lined with attractive houses and shops.

one of the area's finest high streets, lined with attractive 17th- and 18th-century houses, descending steeply to a packhorse bridge over the River Windrush.

The massive, cathedral-like church stands by the river. In the 19th century the church was so badly treated by restorers that an outraged William Morris was provoked into forming the Society for the Protection of Ancient Buildings. However, there is much left to enjoy, including the splendid Renaissance monument to Edward Harman (died 1569), barber and surgeon to Henry VIII, decorated with American Indian figures. For more of Burford's history visit the Tolsey Museum (126 High Street; tel: 01993-823 196; Apr–Oct Mon–Fri, Sun 2–5pm, Sat 11am–5pm; free). The town is popular for its eating places and independent shops, including gift and antique outlets.

Feeding Time

Watching the animals being fed is one of the highlights of a visit to Cotswold Wildlife Park. Go to the Walled Garden to see the photogenic penguins get their daily meals at 11am and 3pm. Feeding the big cats is not at set times but if you are near the lion and leopard enclosure around 4pm you might be lucky. Other feeding highlights are mealtimes for the lemurs (every day at noon) and the giant tortoises.

Above: Humboldt penguin at the Cotswold Wildlife Park.

ⓕ Deadly Deeds at the Hall

The romantic ruins of Minster Lovell Hall are actually shrouded in mystery and concern the fate of Francis, the ninth and final baron. Francis fled after fighting with Richard III at the battle of Bosworth in 1485, never to been seen again, his lands reverting to the crown. In the 18th century a skeleton was unearthed sitting at a table in an underground room. Could this have been Francis?

Above: the ruins of Minster Lovell Hall with the church behind.

WINDRUSH VALLEY

It is worth making a short detour to **Minster Lovell** by following the signs along the A40 4 miles (6.5km) east from Burford. This exceptionally attractive village has a fine Perpendicular church and the ruined 15th-century **Minster Lovell Hall** (daylight hours; see *box, above*). From here, return to Burford.

The Barringtons

West of Burford, the Windrush flows through a series of unspoiled villages. Quarries at Taynton and the Barringtons supplied stone for such notable buildings as Windsor Castle, Blenheim Palace, the crypt of St Paul's Cathedral and several Oxford colleges. To reach Great Barrington, take the main street through Burford, go over the river and take the A424 for Stow-on-the-Wold, shortly taking a left turn to Taynton and on to the beautiful village of Great Barrington.

These villages also supplied the masons to work the stone, one of whom built the back lane from **Great Barrington** downhill to the mill-stream, over the Windrush and up

Below: houses on the Green at Little Barrington.

to the church at **Little Barrington**. Known as Strong's Causeway, the lane was built under the terms of the will of Thomas Strong, a local man who Sir Christopher Wren appointed as his chief mason for the rebuilding of St Paul's Cathedral.

In Great Barrington village turn left at the war memorial and driving downhill note the church; several monuments testify to the sculptors' skills, including those to the Bray children (died 1720) by Christopher Cass, and to Mary, Countess Talbot (died 1787) by Joseph Nollekens. By contrast, Little Barrington's church is a simple Norman building with carvings of Christ in Majesty.

A little further downhill pull over to see the river on the left and note how wild and natural the Windrush looks for much of its course. Several local landowners are committed to wildlife conservation, resulting in a corridor of undrained water meadow 15 miles (24km) in length. Continuing on over the bridge turn left for Little Barrington and its church.

Retrace your route, taking the fork left by the Fox Inn and then continue west along the river through Windrush and on to Sherborne.

Estate Village

At **Sherborne** ❽ (www.national trust.org.uk; open all year; small charge car park donation) the restored 18th-century watermeadows include sluice gates and channels that flood the fields in winter to protect grass from frost damage and thus produce early grazing. There are some excellent marked walks. Sherborne village was built as a model estate village in the mid-19th century, and consists of distinctive rows of identical stone cottages. The main house (in the centre of the village on the left and now apartments) has a magnificently flamboyant facade

Above: eclectic mix of garden ornaments in Sherborne.

(1663). The church alongside contains a cluster of good monuments, including one that features an angel with fashionable décolletage carved by Richard Westmacott in 1791. Continue through the village and at the crossroads take the road south back down to the A40.

Cross over the A40 signposted to **Lodge Park** (tel: 01451-844 130; www.nationaltrust.org.uk; mid-Mar–Oct Fri–Sun 11am–4pm; charge), a rare example of a 17th-century hunting lodge *(see box, p.108)*, beautifully restored by the National Trust. Continue south and take the next left for Aldsworth.

COLN VALLEY

Bibury

Climbing out of the Windrush Valley, cross the bare tops southwards by following the B4425 southwest to rejoin the Coln Valley at **Bibury** ❾, which William Morris called the

ⓕ Watching the Deer

Lodge Park, England's only surviving 17th-century deer course and grandstand for observing the deer, is situated on the Sherborne Estate (see p.107) and was built in 1634 for John 'Crump' Dutton, a Civil War politician. It is set in parkland designed in the 18th century by landscaper Charles Bridgeman and modified into a house in the 19th century. It was bequeathed to the National Trust in 1982 and subsequently restored.

Above: watermeadows at Sherborne, restored in the 18th century.

prettiest village in England (Henry Ford agreed; in the 1920s he tried to buy houses in the village to transport back to America).

Arlington Mill and Trout Farm

The River Coln flows along the main street of Bibury. Entering at the eastern end of the village, the unusually large church stands alongside Bibury Court, built in 1633 (now a hotel, see p.124). Some of the original Saxon church survives, including fragments of cross shaft carved with interlace.

Above: Arlington Row, Bibury..

There is a fine stained-glass window in the chancel by Karl Parsons (1884–1934). Heading west, between the river and the main street, is a green expanse of boggy watermeadow known as Rack Isle. On the left bank, close to the Catherine Wheel pub, are the picturesque Arlington Row cottages, built in 1380 as a monastic wool store. In the 17th century, this was converted into a row of weavers' cottages, and the cloth produced here was sent to Arlington Mill, on the other side of Rack Isle, for fulling (de-greasing). The cloth was hung to dry on timber frames on Rack Isle. Sadly the mill has now closed both as a working concern and a museum.

Barnsley

As you approach **Barnsley** ⑩ on the B4425, you will first skirt the tree-filled grounds of Barnsley Park (open to the public only during the Barnsley Festival in mid-May), before entering the main street of this village, where until quite recently telephone wires, overhead cables and televison aerials were banned as a way of preserving its timeless appearance. The village is famous for **Barnsley House** (through the village and to the left) where the splendid 4-acre (1.6-

hectare) garden created by Rosemary Verey (1918–2001) became one of the most visited and influential in Britain. Her skill was to combine formal design with cottage garden planting, and indeed Prince Charles was so impressed that he invited her to advise him on his garden at Highgrove. Verey's husband, David, who rescued various stone structures from demolished buildings in the area and used them to create gazebos and focal points, created the framework of the garden in the 1960s. Barnsley

House is now an exclusive hotel (see p.123) but the garden is open to the public on selected days and on one Saturday in May to coincide with the flowering of the renowned laburnum walk; or visit when it is open for the National Gardens Scheme (see box p.81). Otherwise, to see the gardens you can book lunch, tea or dinner at the hotel, or go to one of the plays or concerts held in the gardens in summer. Verey's hallmark potager now supplies The Village Pub (see below) in Barnsley with vegetables.

Ⓔ Eating Out

Lechlade

Colleys
High Street; tel: 01367-252 218; www.colleyslechlade.co.uk; Tue–Thu noon–2pm, 6.30pm–9.45pm, Fri–Sat noon–2pm.
During the week Colleys Brasserie and Grill features locally sourced produce at a reasonable price. Colley's Classics – four courses – are available in one sitting on Friday and Saturday night. Good Sunday set lunch. ££

The Trout Inn
Burford Street; tel: 01367-252 313; www.thetroutinn.com; food served Mon–Sat noon–2pm, 7–10pm, Sun noon–2.30pm, 7–9.30pm.
Expect a warm welcome at this popular pub fronting the river. Honest, home-made food includes dishes using local ingredients such as Bibury trout. ££

Eastleach Turville

The Victoria Inn
Tel: 01367-850 277; www.victoriainneastleach.co.uk; food served daily noon–2pm, 7–9pm (Sun dinner only July and Aug).
Beautifully situated, the Victoria is perfect for lunch. Freshly prepared offerings include excellent baguettes, stuffed with classic fillings such as brie and cranberry, but at

heart this is a locals' pub with great beer. £–££

Burford

The Angel
14 Witney Street; tel: 01993-822 714; www.theangelatburford.co.uk; Mon–Sat noon–3pm, 6–9.30pm, Sun noon–4pm, 6.30–8.30pm.
First-class lunches include platters of charcuterie or olives, humous and nuts. There's also an excellent Sunday lunch menu and a set lunch menu for the rest of the week. ££

Huffkins
96–98 High Street; tel: 01993-822 126; www.huffkins.com; Mon–Fri 9am–5pm, Sat 9am–5.30pm, Sun 10am–5pm.
The highlight here must surely be the freshly baked breads handcrafted on site. Also serves soups, sandwiches and scrumptious cakes. £

Barnsley

The Village Pub
Tel: 01285-740 421; www.thevillagepub.co.uk; Mon–Fri noon–2.30pm, 6–9.30pm, Sat noon–3pm, 6–9.30pm, Sun noon–3pm, 6–9pm.
This village pub is not run-of-the-mill. Classic English dishes with an innovative and creative twist feature on the menu. Try the local beef in ale pie or quail Scotch eggs. ££

Travel Tips

Active Pursuits

The terrain of the Cotswolds lends itself to a wide range of activities, from the tranquil sport of fishing to the thrill of mountain biking and kayaking. Walking and cycling are among the most popular pastimes in the region, but there are also plenty of opportunities for golf, horse riding and a variety of water sports.

CHILDREN

Activities catering for children in the Cotswolds range from wildlife attractions for animal lovers, and country parks where they can hunt for fossils, to strenuous activities such as horse riding, cycling and water sports. Many places have adventure playgrounds; one of the best is at Sudeley Castle (see p.66).

CYCLING

Leave the car behind and hit the trail with a day out cycling. Most visitor information centres have details of cycle routes in their areas, some of which can be downloaded from the internet at www.cotswold.gov.uk.

Cotswold Country Cycles

Longlands Farm Cottage, Chipping Campden; tel: 01386-438 706; www.cotswoldcountrycycles.com. Bikes are available for hire on a daily basis or there are specially devised tours for longer trips.

Hartwells Cycle Hire

High Street, Bourton-on-the-Water; tel: 01451-820 405; www.hartwells.supanet.com. With a fleet of more than 40 mountain bikes of all sizes, Hartwells are well set up to supply all the necessary for your cycling trip. Good route maps supplied for half-day, full-day and three- to seven-day tours are available. There is even a tandem for hire.

Previous pages: Arlington Row, Bibury. Left: Sudeley Castle's adventure playground.

Painswick Pedals

Gloucester Road, Painswick; tel: 01452-813 204; www.painswickpedals. co.uk. In the Rococo Gardens; make light work of it and hire an electric assisted bike.

Stratford Bike Hire

Seven Meadows Road, Stratford-upon-Avon; tel: 07711-776 340; www. stratfordbikehire.com. Choose from a cycle tour around Shakespeare's houses and gardens or take a spin down the Stratford Greenway for a traffic-free route (see p.75).

GOLF

The following clubs, all set in scenic escarpment-edge locations, welcome day visitors. Check with the local visitor information centres for more courses.

Cleeve Hill

Cleeve Hill, near Cheltenham; tel: 01242-672 025; www.cleevehillgolf course.co.uk. Set in 1,000 acres (405 hectares) high up on Cleeve Common, this 72 par, heathland course will test your skill.

Cotswold Edge

Wotton-under-Edge; tel: 01453-844 167; www.cotswoldedgegolfclub.org. uk. A challenging, par 71 course, with stunning views across to the Brecon Beacons and Malvern Hills.

Minchinhampton

Minchinhampton; near Stroud; tel: 01453-833 840; www.minchinhamp tongolfclub.co.uk. There are three courses under the clubs banner: the original par 70 Avening Course with a parkland style, the par 71 Chering-ton Course with more of a links feel, and the lovely Old Course (par 71), which was established in 1889 and has a stunning setting right on Minchin-hampton Common.

Painswick

Golf Course Lane; tel: 01452-812 180; www.painswickgolf.com. Great views over the Slad Valley from this fine par 67 course founded in 1891.

RIDING

Off-road horse riding and tuition for all ages and abilities can be found throughout the Cotswolds.

Barton End Stables

Barton End, Nailsworth; tel: 01453-834 915; www.bartonendstables.co.uk.

© Out in the Wild

For something a bit different and to try new green skills, Woodland Ways (tel: 01234 351006 ; www.woodland-ways.co.uk) might be just what you are looking for. Go back to nature by learning the art of bushcraft using natural resources in a sustainable manner. Learn the skills of our ancestors, still used by indigenous peoples around the world. Half- and one-day workshops available as well as longer courses.

Above: learn bushcraft and foraging skills with Woodland Ways.

Approved by the British Horse Society. A friendly place on a family-run farm.

Camp Riding Centre

The Camp, near Stroud; tel: 01285-821 219; www.ridingschoolgloucester shire.co.uk. Scenic rides for all the family. Tuition available.

Hall Place

Noverton Farm, Pear Tree Lane, Prestbury; tel: 01242-241 562; www. passivehorsemanship.com. Teaches 'passive horsemanship', where riders learn to 'listen' to their horse. With horses to suit all abilities, you can try your hand at Western-style riding and learn to love your steed.

Above: the Cotswold Way is the main long-distance footpath running through the region.

WALKING

Visitors to the Cotswolds Area of Outstanding Beauty are spoiled for choice when it comes to walking opportunities – the whole region is criss-crossed with more than 3,000 miles (4,830km) of footpaths and also long, flat canal and river towpaths.

Long-distance footpaths include the Gloucestershire Way, Cotswold Way (see p.53), Oxfordshire Way, Macmillan Way and Monarchs Way. Paths along the river or with river sections include the Thames Path (see p.99), Wysis Way and Windrush Way. The Cotswolds Conservation Board (tel: 01451-862 000; www.escapetothe cotswolds.org.uk) organises an excellent programme of guided walks throughout the year.

You can also download routes online. If you are planning to walk the Cotswold Way, Compass Holidays (tel: 01242-250 642; www.compass-holidays.com) offers an accommodation booking and luggage transfer service.

Most visitor information centres throughout the region have walking routes and trails for both town and country to suit all ages and abilities.

GLIDING AND MICROLIGHTING

To see the Cotswolds from a different angle you might consider taking to the skies in a glider or microlight.

Bristol and Gloucestershire Gliding Club

Near Nympsfield, Stonehouse; tel: 01453-860 342; www.bggc.co.uk. For a bird's eye view of the Cotswolds this club offers lessons, trial flights and group flights.

Kemble Flying Club

Cotswold Airport, Kemble; tel: 01285-770 077; www.kembleflyingclub.co.uk.

Try a bit of microlight training and a trial flight at Kemble, 7 miles (11km) southwest of Cirencester.

FISHING

With a good number of canals, lakes and rivers the Cotswolds is the perfect place for both the new and seasoned angler. The Thames and Coln rivers in particular are good for trout, chubb, grayling and pike. Information on licences, which are legally required, is obtainable from the Environment Agency (www. environment-agency.gov.uk). Commercial fisheries also offer opportunities for angling on lakes.

Bibury Trout Farm

Bibury; tel: 01285-740 215; www. biburytroutfarm.co.uk. Learn all about trout and fishing and get hooked on a new hobby.

Lechlade and Bushyleaze Trout Fishery

Lechlade; tel: 01367-253 266; www. lechladetrout.co.uk. This company offers fly-fishing on the River Leach and on two lakes (Lechlade and Bushyleaze). Tuition is available.

WATER SPORTS

Opportunities exist for sailing, canoeing, kayaking, windsurfing and more.

Cotswold Water Park

Cotswold Water Park Trust Office at Cotswold House, Manor Farm, Down Amprey Estate, near Cirencester; tel: 01793-752 413; www.waterpark.org *(see box, below)*.

South Cerney Outdoor Education Centre

Lake 12, Spine Road; tel: 01285-860 388; www.southcerneyoutdoor.co.uk. If you want more organised water sports, come to this centre, within the Cotswold Water Park. The courses range from one day to full multi-activity weeks and summer camps. You will find all the usual water sports, from windsurfing to canoeing.

Swimming

Should the weather be inclement, there are plenty of indoor activities.

The Cotswold Leisure Centre

Tetbury Road, Cirencester; tel: 01285-654 057; www.cotswold.gov.uk. A 25 metre pool, children's pool and a gym.

Ⓚ Cotswold Water Park

To keep your children active during the holidays, there's a host of opportunities at the Cotswold Water Park *(see above for details)*. With 150 lakes the park is ideal for water sports. There are many land activities as well, including golf, paintballing, aerial adventure and wildlife watching. Within the boundary of the water park is the Cotswold Country Park and Beach (www.cotswoldcountrypark.com) with its man-made beach, bike hire, boat hire, water zorbing and playgrounds.

Above: take a dip in one of the lakes at Cotswold Water Park.

Themed Holidays

The natural beauty of the Cotswolds obviously lends itself to outdoor activities, but there are other options to consider when booking a holiday. Immerse yourself in the Arts and Crafts Movement, paint the beautiful landscape, learn some cookery skills or relax at a spa. For those who like the outdoors but prefer something more sedate, a relaxing canal or riverboat holiday could be the answer, while for those who really want to get down to hard work and help preserve the Cotswolds, a conservation volunteering holiday could be rewarding.

ARTS AND CRAFTS

Be inspired by the movement that brought such illustrious figures as William Morris to the region, learn a new artistic skill or take a course to bring the Cotswold landscape to life through art.

Colour in the Cotswolds

The Coach House, Fraziers Folly, Siddington, nr Cirencester; tel: 01285-651 790; www.colourinthecotswolds.com. With 32 acres (13 hectares) of stunning landscape on your doorstep

Above: learn linocut printing at Colour in the Cotswolds.

this is the place to come for budding artists of the natural world.

Farncombe Estate

Broadway; tel: 03333-456 8580; www.farncombecourses.co.uk. There are day courses and weekend leisure breaks in a raft of arts and crafts subjects from photography to painting and drawing, as well as cake decorating and music.

Stanton Guildhouse

Stanton; tel: 01386-584 357; www.stantonguildhouse.org.uk. The Guildhouse runs summer schools for budding artists and craftspeople. Themes can include stained glass, pottery, woodturning or watercolours.

CHILDREN

What better place to stay with children than on a working farm? Cotswold Farmstay (www.cotswoldfarmstay.co.uk) is made up of farmers from commercial arable or dairy to smallholders with a variety of rare breed animals, who offer holiday accommodation. Another good option for children is the Cotswolds Water Park *(see p.115)*.

COOKING

The Cotswolds is home to several celebrated chefs and outstanding cooks who have left the city for a more idyllic way of life. Take a course and learn from their experience, and by using some of the best local produce on offer in the country, the results should reach high standards.

The Cotswold Chef

Royal Agricultural College, nr. Cirencester; tel: 01285-656 813; www.thecotswoldchef.com. Rob Rees has over 25 years' experience of cooking around the world. His Food Tours or Food Experience packages include visits to local markets and producers. Accommodation can be arranged in the surrounding area.

The Foodworks Cookery School

Colesbourne Park, near Cheltenham; tel: 01242-870 538; www.foodworks cookeryschool.co.uk. This fabulous cookery school is located on the Colesbourne Park estate and offers a wide range of courses for both beginners and experienced cooks.

The Gables School of Cookery

Pipers Lodge, Bristol Road, Falfield; tel: 01454-260 444; www.thegablesschool ofcookery.co.uk. From a four-week residential cookery course to day courses in subjects such as Thai cuisine, bread making or dinner party cooking you are spoilt for choice at The Gables.

SPAS, YOGA AND WELLBEING

The Cotswolds are well endowed with gorgeous country house hotels offering a range of relaxing therapies and beauty treatments. It's also the perfect location for some yoga and meditation retreats.

Spas

Calcot Manor
Nr Tetbury; tel: 01666-890 232; www. calcotmanor.co.uk. Calcot's spa complex has a 16-metre pool, sauna, steam room, outdoor spa pool, exercise room and seven treatment rooms.

Cowley Manor
Cowley, nr Cheltenham; tel: 01242-870 900; www.cowleymanor.com. The C.Side Spa at chic Cowley Manor has two pools, gym, steam room and

Above: the spa pool at Calcot Manor.

sauna plus four treatment rooms, and a pedicure and manicure area.

Yoga and Wellbeing
Holycombe
Whichford, Shipston-on-Stour; tel: 01608-684 239; www.holycombe.com. A place to unwind and recharge, Holycombe is an eco-friendly retreat housed in a delightful Cotswold house offering yoga, pilates and various holistic treatments.

BOATING HOLIDAYS

If you enjoy messing about on the river or canals there are countless companies that offer packages. Check out Cotswold Boat Hire (www.cotswold boat.co.uk) and English Holiday Cruises (www.englishholidaycruises.co.uk).

CONSERVATION

There are several opportunities to use your holiday to help preserve the Cotswold countryside (see p.60). Check out the Cotswold Conservation Board (www.cotswoldsaonb.org. uk); National Trust Working Holidays (www.nationaltrust.org.uk); Cotswold Canals Trust (www.cotswold canals.com); learn the art of dry stone walling (www.dswa.org.uk); or help preserve a Victorian mansion (www. woodchestermansion.co.uk).

Practical Information

All the essential practical information you need to make your trip to the Cotswolds run smoothly.

GETTING THERE

By air

The nearest international airport to the southern Cotswolds is Bristol (tel: 0871-334 4444; www.bristolairport. co.uk), while Birmingham (tel: 0871-222 0072; www.birminghamairport. co.uk) is the closest to the north. Flights from both Europe and the US arrive at both these airports.

By car

From London, the M4 and M40 motorways provide access to the Cotswolds within three hours. The M4 also provides rapid access from Wales, Somerset, Devon and Cornwall, and the M5 from the Midlands and the north.

By coach

National Express operates daily services from all parts of the UK to Cheltenham, calling at Tewkesbury, Evesham, Gloucester, Stroud and Cirencester. Other services operate to Stratford-upon-Avon and Oxford. For bookings and information, tel: 08717-818 178 or visit www.national express.com.

By train

Brunel's Great Western Railway is one of the most scenic lines in southern England, especially the 'Golden Valley' line from Swindon to Cheltenham via Kemble, Stroud, Stonehouse and Gloucester. A line also runs from London Paddington to Worcester via Oxford and Moreton-in-Marsh (journey time to Moreton-in-Marsh, 1 hour 40min). Southwest Trains runs

services to Cheltenham and Gloucester from Wales, the Midlands and southwest England. London Midland trains run to Stratford-upon-Avon from Birmingham, and Chiltern Railways trains arrive there from London Marylebone.

For further information, call National Rail Enquiries (24-hour advance timetable and fare information) on tel: 0845-748 4950 or visit www.national rail.co.uk. You can buy tickets online at www.thetrainline.com.

GETTING AROUND

Public transport

With determination, you can get around the Cotswolds using public transport, but expect to use taxis to reach destinations not on the bus or train routes. Tourist information centres can supply timetables, or you can download a copy of *Explore the Cotswolds by Public Transport* produced by the Cotswolds Conservation Board;

Above: most of the main Cotswold towns, and many of the villages, are served by bus.

www.escapetothecotswolds.org.uk, with information on days out and visitor attractions. Main cities and towns such as Gloucester, Cheltenham and Stratford-upon-Avon have a comprehensive bus network. The Public Transport Information Line (tel: 0871-200 2233) provides a useful service for people wanting public transport timetable information nationally and in and around the Cotswolds.

By car

The ideal way to see the Cotswolds is, without doubt, by car. There are many undiscovered roads that will take you through some of the most stunning scenery, which is only accessible by car or bike. You will find major car hire companies located in Gloucester, Stratford-upon-Avon and Cheltenham but there are more options in Oxford and Bath.

Avis: Gloucester Airport, Gloucester, tel: 0844-544 6114; **Enterprise Rent-A-Car**: 48 Swindon Road, Cheltenham, tel: 01242-514 411, or Unit 8, Swan Trade Centre, Stratford-upon-Avon, tel: 01779-403 920; **Sixt**: Whitworth Court, Baird Road, Gloucester, tel: 0844-499 3399.

By bike

Cycling is popular throughout the Cotswolds and there are many designated cycle paths. Although visitors often bring their own, reliable cycle hire companies can be found throughout the region (see p.112).

By taxi

Stow On The Wold: Cotswold Taxi 4U, tel: 07720-572 420. **Cheltenham**: Cheltenham Taxis, tel: 01242-790 019. **Cirencester**: Radio Cars, tel: 01285-651 117. **Gloucester**: Gloucester Taxi, tel: 01452-341 341. **Moreton-in-Marsh**: Cotswold Taxis, tel: 07710-117 471. **Stratford-**

Above: lace up your boots and ramble through the idyllic countryside.

upon-Avon: A to B Taxis, tel: 01789-415 225. **Tetbury**: Express Taxis, tel: 07858-450 098.

GOING GREEN

Cotswold District Council is committed to green tourism and supports the 'Green Tourism Business Scheme', which encourages visitors to walk, cycle or use public transport while in the region. A selection of leaflets on getting around in the Cotswolds using public transport can be downloaded from www.cotswold.com. Also take a look at The Cotswold Way National Trail website (www.nationaltrail.co.uk), which provides lots of information on walking and public transport in the area.

As part of this scheme the council offers suggestions to local tourism providers to encourage them to find ways of making a positive difference to the environment and local area. For example, ideas for saving water and electricity, buying local produce and helping visitors to consider their method of transport to and from and around the Cotswolds. The website www.green-business.co.uk lists businesses and accommodation options that have been accredited for their efforts in supporting going 'Green'.

FACTS FOR THE VISITOR

Visitors with disabilities

Tourist information centres can help plan your trip and give advice on establishments suitable for visitors with disabilities. For information on places to stay with disabled access in the region check the website www.the-cotswoldsguide.com and the national website www.goodaccessguide.co.uk. Information for travel within the UK for visitors with disabilities can be found on the government website www.gov.uk/transport-disabled.

Sections of footpaths and walking trails in the Cotswolds have been made more suitable for people with mobility problems: surfacing is to a high standard and gates are used instead of stiles wherever possible. The Cotswolds Conservation Board has developed the *Walks on Wheels* guides, a folder of 15 routes designed for families with pushchairs and people in wheelchairs and on powered scooters. The trails are no more than 2½ miles (4km) long and vary from challenging to easier routes. Copies can be downloaded from www.escapetothecotswolds.org.uk.

Emergencies

In emergency, dial 999 for all services; for **local police** tel: 101.
AA Breakdown, tel: 0800-887 766.
RAC Breakdown, tel: 0800-828 282. Always keep the number of your breakdown company handy.

Hospitals: Cheltenham General, Sandford Road, tel: 0300-422 2222; Cirencester Hospital, Tetbury Road, tel: 01285-655 711; Gloucestershire Royal, Great Western Road, Gloucester, tel: 0300-422 2222 or 01242-222 222; Stratford Hospital, Arden Street, Stratford-upon-Avon, tel: 01789-205 831.

Below: paths suitable for wheelchairs are described in *Walks on Wheels*.

Guided tours

To help you make the most of a visit to the Cotswolds, there are many types of organised tours available, including ones on foot, by boat, bus, bike and more. The larger tourist information centres (Cheltenham, Gloucester and Stratford) offer a range of tours.

Cotswold and Gloucestershire Tourist Guides

www.cotswoldguides.org.uk. These are qualified Green Badge Guides, with extensive knowledge and a real enthusiasm for the region. Walking tours of Cheltenham or coach tours for groups can be tailored to suit individual requirements.

Blue Badge Guided Tours

Tel: 024-7669 1212; www.bluebadge touristguide.com. A Blue Badge Guide can show visitors the best that Shakespeare Country has to offer.

City Sightseeing Stratford Tours

Stratford-upon-Avon; tel: 01789-412 680; www.citysightseeingstratford. com. Hop-on hop-off, open-top bus tours of Stratford-upon-Avon departing from the tourist information centre at regular intervals.

Gloucester Civic Trust

St Michael's Tower, The Cross, Gloucester; tel: 01452-526 955; www. gloucestercivictrust.org.uk. Gloucester Civic Trust runs guided walks from April to September around Gloucester's city sights and historic docks.

Bancroft Cruises

Tel: 01789-269 669; www.bancroft cruisers.co.uk. Experience the charm and beauty of Shakespeare country with a guided sightseeing cruise. Departs from the Holiday Inn Stratford.

Above: tempted by cakes in a Stow-on-the-Wold delicatessen.

Opening hours

Most town centre shops generally open Monday to Saturday 9am–5.30pm, sometimes with late-night shopping on Thursday (until around 8.30pm). Several stores also open on Sunday 10am–4pm. Neighbourhood stores and garage forecourt convenience shops often open much longer – 24 hours in many cases.

Tourist information

Bourton-on-the-Water: Victoria Street, Glos GL54 2BU, tel: 01451-820 211; **Burford**: 33a High Street, Burford, Oxfordshire OX18 4QA, tel: 01993-823 558; **Cheltenham**: Art Gallery and Museum, Clarence Street, Glos GL50 3JT, tel: 01242-522 878; **Chipping Campden**: The Old Police Station, High Street, Glos GL55 6HB, tel: 01386-841 206; **Cirencester**: Corinium Museum, Park Street, Glos GL7 2BX, tel: 01285-654 180; **Evesham**: The Almonry Heritage Centre, Abbey Gate, Evesham, Worcestershire WR11 4BG, tel: 01386-446 944; **Gloucester**: 28 Southgate Street, Glos GL1 2DP, tel: 01452-396 572; **Moreton-in-Marsh**: Moreton Area Centre, High Street, Glos GL56 0AZ, tel: 01608-650 881; **Nailsworth**: 4 The Old George, Fountain Street,

Above: Royal Shakespeare Theatre, home to the renowned RSC.

Glos GL6 0BL, tel: 01453-839 222; **Stratford-upon-Avon**: Bridgefoot, Warwickshire CV37 6GW, tel: 01789-264 293; **Stroud**: Subscriptions Rooms, George Street, Glos GL5 1AE, tel: 01453-760 960; **Tetbury**: 33 Church Street, Glos GL8 8JA, tel: 01666-503 552; **Tewkesbury**: Out of the Hat Heritage Centre, 100 Church Street, Glos GL20 5AB, tel: 01684-855 040; **Winchcombe**: Town Hall, High Street, Glos GL54 5LJ, tel: 01242-602 925.

Useful websites:
www.cotswolds.com
www.cotswolds.info
www.visitcotswolds.co.uk
www.thecityofgloucester.co.uk
www.visitcheltenham.co.uk
www.oxfordshirecotswolds.org
www.shakespeare-coutry.co.uk

Entertainment
Most visitors come to the Cotswolds for peace and tranquillity, hence the region does not have much in the way of lively late-night entertainment – most of what exists is found in Cheltenham. That said, the larger towns offer good opportunities to see a play, enjoy a variety of musical performances or catch a film.

Cinemas
Cineworld
The Peel Centre, St Ann Way, Bristol Road, Gloucester and The Brewery, Oxford Passage, St Margaret's Road, Cheltenham; tel: 0871-200 2000; www.cineworld.co.uk (contact details for both cinemas).

Stratford Picturehouse
Windsor Street; tel: 0871-902 5741; www.picturehouses.co.uk/cinema/stratford_upon_avon.

Music and Theatre
The Bacon Theatre
Dean Close School, Shelburne Road, Cheltenham; tel: 01242-258 002; www.bacontheatre.co.uk.

Cheltenham Town Hall and Pitville Pump Room
Imperial Square, Cheltenham; tel: 0844-576 2210; www.cheltenhamtownhall.org.uk.

Everyman Theatre
Regent Street, Cheltenham; tel: 01242-572 573; www.everymantheatre.org.uk.

Playhouse Theatre
Bath Road, Cheltenham; tel: 01242-522 852; www.playhousecheltenham.org.

Gloucester Guidhall
23 Eastgate Street, Gloucester; tel: 01452-503 050; www.gloucester.gov.uk/guildhall.

Kings Theatre
Kingsbarton Street, Gloucester; tel: 01452-300 130; www.kingstheatre.uk2k.com.

Royal Shakespeare Company
Waterside, Southern Lane, Stratford-upon-Avon; tel: 0844-800 1100; www.rsc.org.uk.

Accommodation

The Cotswolds provides a diverse range of accommodation to help make your stay special, from historic luxury hotels in idyllic surroundings to friendly B&Bs, congenial country inns and charming self-catering options.

Accommodation in the Cotswolds can offer competitive prices outside peak times, as bed-and-breakfasts are plentiful and there are numerous hotels and self-catering cottages and farmhouses available. Booking ahead is advised during peak times and at weekends but most other times the supply more than meets the demand. If arriving without accommodation call into the tourist information centre at your chosen destination (see p.121–2), and they will be happy to help you find a room (there may be a small fee).

Price ranges for a hotel room for one night for a double room including breakfast (quoted as a guide only) are as follows:

Above: Barnsley House hotel is surrounded by superb gardens, including formal lawns.

£££	over £150
££	£80–150
£	under £80

SOUTH COTSWOLDS

Abbey Home Farm
Burford Road, Cirencester; tel: 01285-640 441; www.theorganicfarmshop.co.uk.
This is about as green and eco-friendly as you could possibly get, all in a delightful woodland setting. Choose from yurts, huts or a holiday cottage at Abbey Farm. Organic farm shop and café on site. £

Amberley Inn
Culver Hill, Amberley; tel: 01453-872 565; www.theamberleyinn.co.uk.
Minchinhampton Common provides enviable views for this historic inn which retains its original charms. The individual en suite rooms are light and airy with Egyptian cotton linen and home-like comfort. ££

Barnsley House
Barnsley; tel: 01285-740 000; www.barnsleyhouse.com.
Superb but expensive country house hotel set in delightful gardens. Plenty of old features but the rooms are contemporary and stylish with private terraces. The restaurant is classy, and with indulgent extras include the Garden Spa. £££

The Bear of Rodborough
Rodborough Common, Stroud; tel: 01453-878 522; www.cotswold-inns-hotels.co.uk.
In a quiet southwest corner of the Cotswolds, this former 17th-century coaching inn has been beautifully restored to embrace the period features and has sumptuous, individually styled

bedrooms. The newly refurbished Library restaurant is renowned for its excellence. ££

Bibury Court
Bibury; tel: 01285-740 337; www. biburycourt.co.uk.
This glorious Jacobean house fulfils everyone's idea of the perfect Cotswold manor: relax in the oak-panelled drawing room; take tea on the terrace or a stroll in the beautiful grounds. The 18 bedrooms are delightful, all with their own individual features. ££–£££

Burford House Hotel
99 High Street, Burford; tel: 01993-823 151; www.burfordhouse.co.uk.
A peaceful hotel set in a mellow Tudor landmark building on the High Street full of beams and cosy log fires. Each of the unique bedrooms has a lovely bathroom – and some have four-poster beds. Excellent cream teas. ££–£££

Above: cosy Burford House Hotel occupies a Tudor building on the village high street.

Calcot Manor
Tetbury; tel: 01666-890 391; www. calcotmanor.co.uk. Calcot Manor, with its 17th-century farm buildings, has one of the area's most popular restaurants (see p.35) and a superb spa (see p.117). Choose between four-posters and designer comforts, or family rooms and a children's playroom. £££

Cardynham House
Tibbiwell Street, Painswick; tel: 01452-814 006; www.cardynham.co.uk.
Step back in time at this Grade II listed house with a wealth of character evident in all the spacious bedrooms. Breakfast at Cardynham House is a special occasion. ££

The Crown Inn
Frampton Mansell; tel: 01285-760 601; www.thecrowninn-cotswolds.co.uk.
The 12 fresh and well-appointed rooms are housed in an annexe block behind the delightful inn, which dates back to at least 1633. Very warm hospitality in an idyllic Cotswold setting. ££

Crown of Crucis
Ampney Crucis; tel: 01285-851 806; www.thecrownofcrucis.co.uk.
Housed in a former 16th-century inn, set in a tranquil setting overlooking the village cricket pitch and the Ampney Brook, the hotel takes on a country style. All the bedrooms surround a central courtyard. Good food. £–££

The Green Dragon
Cockleford, Cowley; tel: 01242-870 271; www.green-dragon-inn.co.uk.
Well concealed in the tiny lanes between Cowley and Elkstone, this pretty inn is the perfect secluded haven for those who appreciate good food, real ales and comfortable cottage-style accommodation. ££

Above: the entrance to Lords of the Manor Hotel in Upper Slaughter.

Hatton Court
Upton Hill, Upton St Leonards; tel: 01452-617 412; http://hatton-court.co.uk. Country-house hotel ideally located between Gloucester and Painswick on the edge of the Cotswold Escarpment, hence the great views. Rooms are individually styled, blending contemporary decor with traditional comfort, but all are spacious and some have a jacuzzi. £–££

NORTH COTSWOLDS
The Arden Hotel
Waterside, Stratford-upon-Avon; tel: 01789-298 682; www.theardenhotelstratford.com.
Occupying a stunning waterfront setting, the Arden was refurbished and opened as a boutique-style hotel in 2010. It includes the Waterside Brasserie and a champagne bar as well as spacious rooms and suites overlooking the River Avon. £££.

Badger's Hall
High Street, Chipping Campden; tel: 01386-840 839; www.badgershall.com. A warm welcome is assured at this beautiful Cotswold B&B, which oozes character at every turn. The rooms are furnished to a high standard, the

breakfasts are outstanding and there is a superb tearoom on the premises serving home-made treats. ££

The Crown and Trumpet
Church Street, Broadway; tel: 01386-853 202; www.cotswoldholidays.co.uk. Set behind the touristy main street, this pretty, friendly 17th-century pub is for those who like to stay in traditional, no-frills accommodation with good pub grub, and to drink alongside the locals. Two cottages also available for rent. £

The Feathered Nest Country Inn
Nether Westcote; tel: 01993-833 030; www.thefeatherednestinn.co.uk. Nothing disappoints, from the quirky saddles for bar stools to the comfy sofas around an open fire. Attention to detail is superb: complimentary nibbles such as chocolates and fresh fruit in the delightful bedrooms, first-class food, attentive staff and a lovely setting. ££–£££

Lords of the Manor Hotel
Upper Slaughter; tel: 01451-820 243; www.lordsofthemanor.com.
A 17th-century rectory in honey-coloured stone set in parkland with a river meandering through the grounds. With fabulous food and luxury accommodation, this is the perfect choice for imagining you are lord or lady of the manor. £££

The Lygon Arms
High Street, Chipping Campden; tel: 01386-840 318; www.lygonarms.com. A magnificent 16th-century coaching inn renowned as much for its restaurant as for its roaring log fires and comfortable bedrooms, where traditional features such as wooden beams and Cotswold stone have been retained. ££

Above: Mercure Cheltenham Queen's.

Mercure Cheltenham Queen's
Promenade, Cheltenham; tel: 01242-307 800; www.mecure.com.
If you want Regency splendour in the heart of town, the Queen's won't disappoint you. It's in a perfect location for shopping, restaurants and bars. The rooms are contemporary and many have views of the gardens. There is a good buffet breakfast. ££

Redesdale Arms Hotel
High Street, Moreton-in-Marsh; tel: 01608-650 308; www.redesdalearms.com.
A stalwart of Moreton for some 200 years, this traditional stone hotel has some contemporary touches. Nicely sized bedrooms with attractive country furnishings in the main building and converted stables. Eleven new boutique rooms were added in 2012, some with private garden. ££

Stow Lodge Hotel
The Square, Stow-on-the-Wold; tel: 01451-830 485; www.stowlodge.co.uk.

Centrally located overlooking the market square, this old manor house has stunning gardens where guests can relax. It has built up a fine reputation with many repeat customers. ££

Stratford Limes
41 Main Street, Tiddington; tel: 01789-290 210; www.stratfordlimeshotel.com.
A flat 25-minute walk into the centre of Stratford, for those wanting to stay away from the hustle and bustle, this fresh, stylish accommodation has a pleasant courtyard garden and plenty of parking. £–££

Three Ways House
Mickleton; tel: 01386-438 429; www.threewayshousehotel.com.
Just off the tourist trail this attractive hotel is best known for its Pudding Club. This theme is humorously reflected in the gorgeous bedrooms, which go by such splendid names as Spotted Dick and Custard and the Chocolate Suite. A delightful place to stay. ££–£££

ACCOMMODATION WEBSITES
Guest houses/B&Bs/Hotels
www.the-cotswolds.org
www.accommodationcotswolds.com
www.visitcotswolds.co.uk

Self-catering
National Trust properties converted into self-catering accommodation: www.nationaltrustcottages.co.uk.

Other self-catering agencies include:
www.country-accom.co.uk
www.cottageinthecountry.co.uk
www.holidaycottages.co.uk/cotswolds
www.manorcottages.co.uk.

Camping
www.cotswoldyurts.co.uk

Index

Credits

Insight Great Breaks The Cotswolds
Written by: Jackie Staddon and Hilary Weston
Project Editor: Catherine Dreghorn
Copy-editor: Stephanie Smith
Picture Manager: Zoë Goodwin
Maps: APA Cartography Department
Production: Tynan Dean and Rebeka Davies
Publishing Manager: Rachel Fox
Series Editor: Sarah Clark

All Pictures APA/Tony Halliday except:
Alamy 7B, 18T, 20/T, 27L, 29B, 34/T, 43, 44T, 45B, 46B, 53B, 54T, 57B, 60, 61M/T, 72B, 75, 76, 79B, 86T, 90, 95/T, 98, 102B, 104T, 105B, 108B, 110/111, 112, 113B, 115, 118, 120, 121, 123, 124, 125, 126; Elliot Brown 122; Colour in Cotswolds 116; Courtesy Calcot Manor 117; APA/Lydia Evans 4BR/TL, 5TR, 10BL, 22T, 67/T, 77, 78, 80, 81T; Fotolibra 46T; Courtesy Hook Norton Brewery 11; iStockphoto 5BL, 8, 9, 36T, 66B, 74T, 86M, 119; Pictures Colour Library 79T, 86/87, 86B; APA Corrie Wingate 26

Cover pictures by: (front) Fotolia
(All others) Corrie Wingate/Apa Publications

CONTACTING THE EDITORS: As every effort is made to provide accurate information in this publication, we would appreciate it if readers would call our attention to any errors and omissions by contacting:
Apa Publications, PO Box 7910, London SE1 1WE, England.
Email: insight@apaguide.co.uk
Information has been obtained from sources believed to be reliable, but its accuracy and completeness, and the opinions based thereon, are not guaranteed.

© 2014 APA Publications (UK) Ltd.
Second Edition 2014
Printed in China by CTPS

Map Production: Phoenix Mapping; Mapping contains Meridian 2 data © Crown copyright and database right and other elements © OpenStreetMap and contributors, CC-BY-SA.

Worldwide distribution enquiries:
APA Publications GmbH & Co. Verlag KG (Singapore branch), 7030 Ang Mo Kio Ave 5, 08-65 Northstar @ AMK
Singapore 569880
apasin@singnet.com.sg
Distributed in the UK by:
Dorling Kindersley Ltd, a Penguin Group company, 80 Strand, London WC2R 0RL
sales@uk.dk.com
Distributed in the United States by:
Ingram Publisher Services
1 Ingram Boulevard, PO Box 3006, La Vergne, TN 37086-1986
ips@ingramcontent.com